# THAT WAS THE
# CHURCH, THAT WAS

# THAT WAS THE CHURCH, THAT WAS

*How the Church of England lost the English people*

## ANDREW BROWN AND LINDA WOODHEAD

B L O O M S B U R Y

LONDON · OXFORD · NEW YORK · NEW DELHI · SYDNEY

Bloomsbury Continuum
An imprint of Bloomsbury Publishing Plc

50 Bedford Square
London
WC1B 3DP
UK

1385 Broadway
New York
NY 10018
USA

www.bloomsbury.com

Bloomsbury, Continuum and the Diana logo are trademarks of Bloomsbury
Publishing Plc

First published 2016

Andrew Brown and Linda Woodhead, 2016

Andrew Brown and Linda Woodhead have asserted their rights
under the Copyright, Designs and Patents Act, 1988, to be
identified as Authors of this work.

British Library Cataloguing-in-Publication Data
A catalogue record for this book is available from the British Library.

Library of Congress Cataloguing-in-Publication data has been applied for.

ISBN: HB: 978-1-4729-2164-2
ePDF: 978-1-4729-2166-6
ePub: 978-1-4729-2165-9

6 8 10 9 7 5

Printed and bound in Great Britain by CPI Group (UK) Ltd, Croydon CR0 4YY

MIX
Paper from
responsible sources
FSC
www.fsc.org   FSC® C013604

To find out more about our authors and books visit www.bloomsbury.com.
Here you will find extracts, author interviews, details of forthcoming events
and the option to sign up for our newsletters.

# CONTENTS

*Do not I hate them, O LORD, that hate thee? And am not I grieved with those that rise up against thee? I hate them with perfect hatred: I count them mine enemies.*

PSALM 139:21-2

*Truth is a naked and open day-light, that doth not show the masks and mummeries and triumphs of the world, half so stately and daintily as candle-lights.*

FRANCIS BACON

*What are the roots that clutch, what branches grow Out of this stony rubbish?*

T. S. ELIOT, *THE WASTE LAND*

# 1

# The prospect from Windsor

In the autumn of 1986 the Church of England was still run by men who smoked pipes. Archbishop Robert Runcie stood out as rather dandyish among them because he didn't smoke, and because he liked his spectacles to have light metal frames, instead of the weighty, emphatic dark frames that most bishops wore to read and which gave a deliberative emphasis to their pronouncements. There seemed nothing exotic at all about them when a small group gathered in one of the guest houses within the curtain wall of Windsor Castle.

Andrew leaned on the battlements with the then Archbishop of York, John Habgood, outside the library that Henry VI had built, and looked across the suburban river valley towards Datchet. The Archbishop gestured to the east, at his old school, which Henry VI had also founded: the chapel of Eton was still one of the largest buildings in the view. 'They can't teach history properly there any more,' he said. 'Otherwise Charles Moore would know better.'

Moore was then the editor of the *Spectator*, a young man whose ambition was so obvious and at the same time so tightly controlled that he seemed to move around inside constricting armour, like the tin man in *The Wizard of Oz*. He had been Andrew's employer, more or less, for the previous two years and he was a very serious Christian who was determined to prevent the Church of England from ordaining women priests. In the event, he would become a Roman Catholic rather than remain in a church that did so. He would end up as editor of the *Daily Telegraph* and biographer of Margaret Thatcher but at the time he thought a lot about saving English Christianity.

Habgood was one of the chief enemies of the two oppositional groups within the Church. The conservative Anglo-Catholics hated him because he was a fairly unambiguous supporter of women priests; the evangelicals because he had supported and protected David Jenkins, the bishop of Durham, who was widely supposed to believe nothing at all of traditional Christianity. Mrs Thatcher and her circle hated him because he was an Etonian who believed in the order of society they wanted to overthrow.

There were women present in St George's House but almost all of them were wives, or in one case the daughter, of a bishop. Andrew thinks he remembers one woman theologian speaking but that may have been from a later meeting. In any case, what had brought this meeting together was politics of the old-fashioned sort. It was meant to heal some of the wounds that had been opened within the Establishment by the publication the previous year of *Faith in the City*, the Church of England's report on Thatcher's progress. Alongside John Habgood and David Jenkins, there was a cluster of

Conservative politicians, among them John Selwyn Gummer, then a minister but outside the cabinet, and Ralph Harris, who ran and had founded one of the think-tanks which was assailing the moral and intellectual foundations of the welfare state. To balance them came the Labour intellectual Raymond Plant. His short talks were actually entirely devastating to the intellectual basis of the neoliberal programme; they made as much impression on the politicians as a flea might make on a tank.

Andrew came there as a journalist, mildly bewildered but thoroughly confident. For most of his life, Christianity had been neither sensible nor particularly repulsive. He had been given the kind of English middle-class education in which mild doses of conventional piety served, like cowpox, to inoculate against disfiguring enthusiasms. The background presence of Protestant Christianity was taken for granted. It might not be what you believed in, but it supplied a solid point of reference for what you didn't believe.

Hymns, prayers, and dust motes dancing in the light from chapel windows were all as much part of schooling as muddy winter afternoons on the sports field. In fact they had more point to them than sport. At prep school Andrew learnt a lot of Christian poetry by heart and sang hymns every day beneath a huge mural depicting the green hills of heaven, peopled by a muscular race who had obviously sprung there fresh from a dip in the Cherwell. When he was eleven, an evangelical beat group – they called themselves the Crossbeats – played for the boys beneath that mural and changed his life. It was the first time he had ever heard an electric guitar close up. The words were gibberish but the banging certitude of the instruments showed him bliss. He felt his heart, like Wesley's, strangely warmed. He has never entirely lost the conviction that redemption, salvation and justification are really musical terms.

At Marlborough, a public school founded for the sons of the clergy, one of the housemasters would explain in interviews with parents that his faith gave him confidence that he could help the boys through their troubles. This was not apparent to the boys themselves. What Andrew remembers is the rank miasma of testosterone and snobbery that rose from 800 adolescent boys confined with 15 girls. Great efforts were made there to bring Christianity up to date. The headmaster told a gathering of senior boys that masturbation was not a sin: he did it himself sometimes when his wife was away, just as he ate fish and chip suppers when she was not there to cook for him.

Until he became a religious correspondent, Andrew had met very few Christians who were not either sinister or ludicrous. This didn't really matter, because Christianity was so deeply embedded in his culture. The Book of Common Prayer was the foundation of the language that everyone spoke and read. It seemed to him that its cadences were available to every writer and its allusions common to every Englishman.

That sense seems absurd now and was anachronistic even then, but it's not certain that any of us yet knew that. One of the more curious aspects of the rage with which the English ruling class turned against the institutions that had nourished it – and in this respect the Thatcherites were quite as destructive as the left-wing rebels of the 1960s – was that none of the attackers truly believed that the Establishment they raged against was really vulnerable.

None of us could foresee a time when England would be governed quite without the wise counsel of pipe-smoking men in heavy spectacles.

The background of the pipe-smokers and their church wasn't just the British Empire. That still bestowed a certain confidence, but was being rather hurriedly consigned to history. It was the experience of the Second World War, and the bright hopes that followed it, which inspired and preoccupied them. Empire had given way to post-war Britain, a society rationally organized for the good of all, and run by benevolent educated men. The welfare state had been in many ways a creation of the Church of England: several of its architects were devout Anglicans, it had donated its hospitals, schools and other institutions, and the whole project was deeply influenced by the thought of William Temple, Archbishop of Canterbury in the 1940s.

The divisiveness of the Thatcher years seemed particularly frightening to the Church of England because it threatened the idea of England as an organic whole which could be served in all its parts by the Church. A great many of the clergy were animated by a sense that the bishop in his palace had a spiritual connection with the miners in their striking villages, and a duty to speak for them. Disconcertingly, Conservative Christians felt that they too held the moral and theological higher ground – that the Church had sold out to do-gooding worldliness and outmoded economics. They acted like the inheritors of another long-standing Anglican tradition: the one that says in the end it is the laypeople, in Parliament, who decide what bishops should believe and do. Moore and Gummer thought of themselves as defenders of the Church of England, even as they plotted in every way to rip it apart if it did not do as they wished.

So the two sides came to Windsor to thrash out their disagreements.

St George's House was a wonderful retreat for the Establishment. At seminars in the Library the guests could listen to philosophers and scientists explaining their work, and on one occasion to the Duke of Edinburgh explaining their own work right back to them. The front door of the main house opened into a courtyard which had been old to the Tudors. Within the house were smaller rooms for discussion in groups of eight or ten, all furnished as sitting rooms with comfortable chintzy sofas and armchairs and low, dark wooden coffee tables rather than anything that would suggest formal learning. There was certainly nothing so vulgar as a whiteboard or a screen on the wall.

The comfort and confidence of established power seeped out from the comfortable sofas up through the comfortable bottoms of the men who sat in them. One moment made this completely clear. In the course of a long wrangle about women priests St Paul's views on male headship came up. All the men present agreed that these were risible (no women ventured an opinion) but after dilating on the backwardness and ignorance of that part of Paul's teaching for some time, David Edwards rebuked a more liberal colleague, 'Nevertheless, I do find Paul very helpful', which put the apostle firmly in his place.

Edwards was then as close to the centre of the Church of England as any man could be. Learned, funny and fluent, he had written an urbane preface to *Crockford's Clerical Directory* for the preceding ten years. There might be small barbs in the subtext but they could only be felt by people who knew what he was talking about. An outsider or a mere journalist could not have understood them at all; the Establishment knew how to murder with manners. He had also written a serene history of English Christianity. He would never be a bishop, since he had defied the rules to marry a divorced woman in his own cathedral; he was in favour of women priests, and although he loved the language of the Book of Common Prayer he had no sympathies for the traditionalists who felt it should be used more. 'I often wonder where these people were who now lament the disappearance of Matins. They certainly never showed up at 7:30 in the morning when I was celebrating it for years, and neither did anyone else.'

So this was the ruling elite of the Church of England. They worked in an institution which could plausibly claim to be unchanged in its essentials for 1,500 years. Habgood was the 95th Archbishop of York, Jenkins the 75th bishop of Durham. The latter had been the subject of an unusual campaign of public mockery and vilification since his appointment was announced, and part of him just loved it. He did not believe in the Virgin Birth and said so; he did not believe that Jesus had walked on water and he said that, too. 'The resurrection was not just a conjuring trick with bones,' he had said when he was questioned about his beliefs, and this came out in the media, of course, as 'Bishop compares resurrection to "a conjuring trick with bones"'. When York Minster was struck by lightning three days after his consecration, and badly damaged by the subsequent fire, it was almost irresistible to suppose that God might have been sending the Church a message, and quite a lot of people believed that seriously.

In many ways, Jenkins was the most important bishop in England at that time. In the public imagination he stood for unbelievers everywhere. He was The Bishop Who Didn't Believe A Word Of It, and for about twenty years after he retired, the post of 'bishop of Durham' was filled in the popular imagination by the clergyman who knew it was all nonsense. This was a caricature which captured something enormously important about the Church of England: that a vital part of it wasn't much concerned with anything that could be pinned down in words on a witness stand. This was often described as liberalism or indifference, but it was not. At its best it expressed a profound faith in symbols and ritual, and a distrust of words to convey what could be known of God.

Jenkins was a man to some extent intoxicated by his own cleverness. He knew he could always rephrase any belief into something else: decades later, when he had been diagnosed with dementia, Andrew ate lunch with him. The disease, as it often does, had washed away the inessential features of his personality. What remained was benevolence, an expectation of being loved, and an unshakeable faith in his own powers.

His confidence was at its height in the late 1980s. After the furore stirred up by his views on the resurrection he had rescued himself in the opinion of the Church by a passionate speech to the General Synod studded with quotable insults and condescension: 'I realise it is stupid and foolish of me to attempt mystical theology in a debate in Synod,' he said. His evangelical opponents held a view of miracles which 'imply[ed], if not portray[ed], a God who is at best a cultic idol and at worst the very devil'. No one had understood what he was saying but everyone was convinced that he meant it and he left listeners with the impression that they had overheard a humble man wrestling with his God.

Habgood, the other champion of liberalism, had a very different style. His imprecisions were willed. He was vague with precision and subtlety, as shown by his stock reply to crank letters: 'Thank you for your letter, which I will read with the attention it deserves.' But this steely, careful style, in which what was not said was quite as important as what was, lacked emotional warmth. The man himself did not. Behind the awkward Etonian scientist (he had a doctorate in frog biology) was a capacity for real sympathy, but he did not think this was something that belonged in public life.

Had you asked, back then, what the threats were to the future of the Church of England, there would have been no doubt at all: the main one was the failure of politicians to comprehend its importance, and the next was the management of women's ordination.

The real storm that would soon break over their heads, and the depth of hatred that some evangelicals nurtured against the liberal establishment gathered in Windsor Castle, were both entirely invisible. A threat from Eton could be discerned from the battlements of Windsor Castle; no one could see that a dangerous attack might come from places like Datchet, where people were proud to vote for Margaret Thatcher and were worried about gays.

Adherence to the Prayer Book had been the test of Anglicanism in the days when the Church was wholly established as the religious expression of the political project of Englishness. Deriving as it did from the Elizabethan settlement, it sought to include parties and persons of very diverse views in a single religious establishment, and its formulations of doctrine were couched in studiously ambiguous terms. England moved decisively away from this kind of theocratic self-understanding during the nineteenth century: first Catholics, then 'dissenters' (members of the 'free' Protestant churches other than the Church of England), Jews and even atheists were admitted to Parliament. If Anglicanism was no longer bound to participation in a particular political system, it needed some other, more explicit and perhaps confessional self-understanding. This took an unexpected form, which the empire made credible: Anglicanism was presented as a theological and political middle way between Catholicism and Calvinism, a global model of reasonable and undogmatic Christianity which trod a path between the extremes of Rome and Geneva. Anglicans had bishops just like Catholics, but no troublesome Pope, and cathedrals purged of idolatrous tat, but still with wonderful choirs. They had the Bible, but they also had brains, and they thought that God approved of them exercising these even in relation to His Holy Scriptures.

Hence the widespread confidence that everyone would be Anglican if only they had the good fortune to understand the advantages of an English perspective. In the first half of the century it allowed Anglicans as various and distinguished as T. S. Eliot, Dorothy Sayers, W. H. Auden and C. S. Lewis to feel that they were all practising 'mere Christianity', in Lewis's phrase, and that Rome had too much ornament, while the low churches had too little beauty, and both had too little reason. Anglicanism was the enemy of tyranny and fanaticism, and the guarantor of freedom combined with duty.

The sense of being a chosen people, with a religion which was the natural engine and ally of civilized progress, was the perfect accompaniment to imperial expansion and confident modernization. 'The great social forces which move onwards in their might and majesty are marshalled on our side,' said Gladstone. This calm confidence survived the experience of two world wars, reinforced by victory, and even managed to take the transition to post-war welfare Britain in its stride: here was a project in which the religious and the secular, the scientific and the ethical, could work in harmony to forge a perfect modern, democratic society which would steer another middle course, this time between the worst extremes of both communism and capitalism.

In the Church itself, and particularly among the Anglo-Catholic clergy, there was a really deep and sincere hope that the Roman Catholic Church would see the error of its ways and understand that Anglicans were Catholics too, who disagreed only about the role of the Pope. At some stage soon enough, the Roman Catholic Church would accept that Anglican priests were real Catholic priests – something that Pope Leo had explicitly denied in 1896 – and after that the two Churches would graciously unite. So in the idea of union with Rome a great principle was at stake. Women were in an important sense irrelevant, and their demands for ordination were not the important thing. What mattered to these opponents of women priests was whether one group of men would be accepted by another one.

These hopes of a union with Rome were of course entirely illusory. Rome could never have offered any terms that were acceptable to the majority of Anglican clergy; in any case, in a country where people are free to switch religion, the whole notion of corporate reunion is curiously outmoded. If you want to become a Catholic or an Anglican, you can just drive to a different church on Sunday. Of course, it does not seem that way to the clergy, for whom a change of theological opinion is also a change of pension provider. But for the great majority of churchgoers the question of church unity is just not very interesting. When finally the rump of Anglo-Catholic resisters managed to get from Rome the deal they had intrigued after for decades – a special order of married priesthood, rather grandly entitled the 'Personal Ordinariate of our Lady of Walsingham' – only about a hundred clergy out of over sixteen thousand left for Rome; after decades of priming their congregations for this momentous event, each one brought on average a congregation of five laypeople with him.

But the prospect of corporate reunion managed to keep the old sense of Anglican importance going, even when it had become patently absurd. It was always discussed as if two similar bodies were merging. That meant, obviously, that they would be two bodies with an all-male priesthood and a similar claim to have bishops descended through a line of laying on of hands all the way from the original apostles. Less obviously but more dishonestly, it suggested the two Churches were rather alike, with similar centralized means of making and enforcing decisions. Since it was one of the founding principles of the family of churches around the world derived from the Church of England and in communion with it – the so-called 'Anglican Communion' – that no one of its constituent churches could bind any other, this required a certain amount of sleight of hand. It was also untrue of the Church of England, which had been fine-tuned to ensure that power was delicately balanced between its constituent parts. The gathering in Windsor was evidence enough of that.

One of the extraordinary features of the constitutional establishment of the Church of England was that it put laypeople in final control. The monarch is the Supreme Governor, even though it is felt to be a solecism to mention it. As the powers of the monarchy had waned, Parliament and politicians had retained control over appointments, and Parliament could and sometimes did interfere in liturgical and other matters. The bishops and deans who assembled for Andrew's weekend in Windsor were joined by politicians not just because they represented the government with which the Church was having a misunderstanding. They were also there as power brokers in their own right in the Church.

Direct Parliamentary control of the Church of England had been gradually diluted in the course of the twentieth century, and in 1970 it was largely replaced by a curious and partly elected body called the General Synod. This could make laws ('measures'), and send them up to Parliament, where a committee might accept or reject them but no longer had powers to modify them. The Synod was split into three 'Houses', of Clergy, Laity, and Bishops, and in its early decades it was quite common for secular politicians with strong Anglican convictions to get themselves elected to the Synod's House of Laity as well. John Selwyn Gummer was the most prominent Conservative to do this, and Frank Field the most important Labour MP. These men seemed to be real power brokers, not least to themselves.

But the Synod, though it might propose laws, had almost no financial power in the Church. It raised no money and set no budgets, although the clergy could and did vote themselves generous remunerations and pension schemes that would lead to a financial crisis. The people who thought they ran the Church were still the bishops. Jenkins and Habgood in particular had a profound scorn for the Synod, for it was lay activists there who had tried to prevent Jenkins' consecration. To both men it was an important point of principle that bishops and dons should be the judges of orthodoxy. Neither had any inkling then of the revolt that was being plotted against them, nor of the profound changes taking place in British society, both of which would damage such enlightened paternalistic rule beyond repair. Over the next three decades the Church of England would lose half its active and nominal members, and for the first time ever a majority of British people came to say they had 'no religion' rather than identify as Christian.

Never again would it be possible for men to stand on the battlements of Windsor Castle and survey with such confidence the state of the Church and nation stretched out below.

# 2

# Cuddesdon: where the mild things are

Even at the time, everyone knew that 1989 would be a year for the history books, but the extent to which it proved to be a hinge only became clear later. Along with the fall of the Berlin Wall went the Cold War and all it had meant in terms of Soviet-style communism and the repression of religious and ethnic identities. These now bubbled to the surface, together with new migrations of people – sprung by choice as well as coercion. Both began to change the complexion of Europe. American-style consumer capitalism, already boosted by the policies of Reagan and Thatcher, went into overdrive, and the benevolence of the state was challenged by a new cult of believers who thought that the market was a more effective means of generating freedom, prosperity and peace.

In Britain, it led to the definitive end of the post-war consensus. Massive upheaval and reform took place in all the institutions which had been most bound up with it: the civil service, nationalized industries, political parties, local councils, trades unions, the NHS, schools, universities and the police. Not even the royal family would be untouched.

Morals changed too, in a revolution which had begun in the 1960s but become mainstream by the late 1980s. It wasn't just about sexual liberation, it was about freedom on a much grander scale. The pool of people who felt they had voice, choice and a right to participate expanded outwards from the old tight-knit circle of *les grands décisionaires* – the 'men who ran things' – and cascaded down the social classes. It then widened to include people of different races, women, the disabled, gay people and children. Deference became a thing of the past, and paternalism was despised. No one now wanted to sit passively and be told what to do, whether by doctors or dons. 'Chairmen' became 'chairs', 'comrades' became 'colleagues', 'patients' and 'passengers' became 'customers'. More Britons than ever before were affluent, well educated, widely travelled, healthy and long-lived.

So great were these changes they even registered on the radar of demographers, those languid readers of spreadsheets who monitor only the fundamental upheavals in human population. They called what was happening a 'second demographic transition' characterized by rising life expectancy and falling fertility and marriage rates. Behind it lay a vast and historically unprecedented change in women's status. For the first time, they were being routinely educated to the same levels as men and entering the workforce in similar numbers. It turned out that once they had the choice and the means, they proved more likely to get divorced and less likely to get married or have children. They were out of the doll's house, and never going back.

Had it not been for migrants, the British government would have started fretting about an ageing and dwindling population. But the rate and scale of migration changed all that. At the start of the 1980s it was still race which was the hot issue, and it was colour racism which gave rise to riots like those in Brixton. But in 1989 it was an angry Islam which forced itself on public attention in Britain when some Muslims in Bradford organized a public incineration of Salman Rushdie's novel *The Satanic Verses*, and Ayatollah Khomeini of Iran issued a fatwa ordering Muslims to kill the author.

By 2001, when a question about religion was included on the general Census for the first time, 72 per cent of the population still identified as Christian, but almost 6 per cent identified with a non-Christian religion (half with Islam), 15 per cent declared no religion, and 8 per cent didn't answer. The 'nones' were mostly younger, and other surveys suggested the Census was undercounting them.

These monumental changes were felt at Ripon College Cuddesdon with about as much force as the gentle breezes which stirred the trees around it. Cuddesdon was one of the most prestigious of the Church of England's training colleges for clergy. Linda, fresh out of Cambridge University, was appointed there as Tutor in Doctrine and Ethics in 1988.

Cuddesdon's relative isolation, both literally and metaphorically, was deliberate. Built in the latter part of the nineteenth century in arts-and-crafts-gothic, and situated in a tiny village, the College had the isolated air of an asylum or minor public school. Its location on top of a steep hill six miles from Oxford meant that the city was near enough to tantalize, but out of the reach of all but the keenest cyclists. The College's high-minded Victorian founders, influenced by the Oxford Movement, wanted to separate clergy from the world so that they could be 'formed' as God's own professionals. Until then clergy, often second and third sons of wealthy families, had roistered their way through Oxford or Cambridge, just like their social peers, before seeking a 'living' – a church with vicarage and land attached. They tended to be worldly men who undertook spiritual duties. The founders of Cuddesdon wanted to produce spiritual men who undertook worldly duties. They designed something austere, monastic and set apart where new-model clergy could enjoy the social and educational advantages of Oxford without being corrupted by its worldliness.

This tendency to enjoy your own cake while looking down on other cake-eaters is just one of the marks of the clergy, particularly senior ones, which can be traced back to the way in which they were trained. Another is party spirit. Cuddesdon was a 'liberal Catholic' College, having been formed out of the merger of a modernist one – Ripon Hall – and an Anglo-Catholic one, Cuddesdon College. There were and still are other, quite separate, colleges for evangelicals and conservative evangelicals. In Oxford, for example, there was, besides Cuddesdon, Wycliffe Hall for evangelicals, and St Stephen's House ('Staggers') for Anglo-Catholics. Other colleges were dotted around the country, with Oak Hill College in north London (motto: 'Be Right and Persist') generally the choice of the most hard-line conservative evangelicals.

At its core, 'liberal' meant believing in human dignity and freedom and the free exercise of the mind. Liberals thought that the search for truth was entirely compatible with the spiritual life, since God was to be worshipped in Spirit and Truth. This was the basic stub of liberalism, to which other theological or political elements were added in a great variety of ways. This is also why there could be liberal Catholics as well as liberal evangelicals, although the latter were rarer. Among the ranks of ordinary Anglicans, liberalism was as much a temper and way of life as a belief system – and most ordinary Anglicans were rather liberal. Whereas evangelicals set store by a small set of central beliefs which they could happily recite, and Anglo-Catholics put their faith in rituals and ceremonies, liberals were marked by the virtues they espoused, including a general niceness and concern to help others. Liberal reticence to proclaim their faith owed less to lack of conviction than to a concern not to embarrass or coerce anyone. This tendency was part and parcel of the English character, but to evangelicals it looked like weakness.

As well as inducting clergy into parties, theological colleges immersed them in the hierarchical system of clerical power and patronage. The fine gradations of clergy rank, together with their 'temporalities', had always been a perfect imitation of the English class system and, at the upper echelons of senior clergy, remained so. Even though differentials in housing and stipends had been abolished for the ranks of ordinary clergy in a rush of post-war egalitarian enthusiasm, senior clergy retained fine gradations of status, epitomized by housing which ascended from stockbroker-belt suburban for assistant bishops to grand palaces for the top-ranked bishops and archbishops.

At the heart of the process of 'preferment' was a system of personal patronage which was still very much alive and intact. Clergy advanced by winning favour from their superiors in sometimes mysterious and unaccountable ways. The process was set in motion from the moment you put yourself forward for ordination, for which you needed the support of a sponsoring bishop. It continued in theological college where the College Principal was your immediate patron. The trick was always to attract attention of the right kind and correct amount. It was a difficult balancing act. The ordinand who failed to pay his bar bills and topped off a late-night party by throwing plates around the dining hall Greek-wedding-style attracted too much attention of the wrong sort. But the quiet one who got respectable marks and caused no trouble was in danger of being overlooked and sent to a parish no one wanted.

The best method was to develop a pastoral problem of just the right degree of seriousness to interest the Principal. It should be neither so grave as to cast doubt on your sanity or moral character, nor so trivial that he felt you were wasting his time. It should render you vulnerable, not certifiable. Getting it right could catapult an aspiring ordinand from virtual invisibility to favoured status by way of just a few sessions of intense pastoral counselling.

The patronage system had the effect of blanketing Cuddesdon in a damp mist of low-level anxiety and mistrust. Things were made worse by the way in which power was exercised in the Church – mostly kept under wraps, but occasionally bursting out in vigorous and unexpected ways. Only the more experienced and mature, or confident and bouncy – like Giles Fraser, later to become famous for resigning from St Paul's Cathedral over the Occupy protest – remained unscathed. Confidence, class and manliness helped. Those with self-doubt and 'issues' suffered most. It was a system that encouraged deference and discouraged stepping out of line, and it was harshest on those whose personal lives didn't fit the preferred mould of married with children.

The situation was exacerbated by the fact that staff and students lived in close proximity. The single ones huddled in quasi-monastic cells separated by thin walls and connected by long corridors leading to shared bathrooms. Everyone met several times a day for meals and chapel. It rubbed the boundaries of individual self-containment red-raw, and made it virtually impossible to do anything in private. To manage to do so for any length of time merely compounded the offence. On learning about a particularly lengthy and well-concealed gay relationship, for example, the Principal exclaimed in moral outrage: 'they've been laughing behind my back the whole time', as if this had been the uppermost thing in the malefactors' minds even in the throes of passion.

The weekly staff meeting was a major intersection in the branching network of College surveillance. The main business appeared to be gossip with intent, and it could last for hours. One member of staff, a cheerful American with limited interest in the student psyche, used to get so bored that he would amuse himself by making the table rise slightly and wobble on his knees as if in a séance. Every week there would be 'pastoral problems' to discuss. It was a competitive business, and the prize went to the staff member who could reveal the biggest student secret – which everyone then pretended they had known all along. Damage in childhood, secret affairs, depressions and traumas – each carried a certain unspoken allocation of points.

The justification for all this was the annual report which had to be written about each student. These were written by individual tutors like Linda, and sent via the Principal to the student's 'DDO' (Diocesan Director of Ordinands) and ultimately to the bishop. Winning the favour of the Principal, DDO and bishop was vital to landing a good curacy, followed by a good parish, followed by preferment. Writing these reports was the most miserable, time-consuming and stressful part of the job at Cuddesdon. When Linda left to become a lecturer at Lancaster University, she gazed over the heads of the undergraduates in her classes with a sense of joyful liberation: 'Sleep with whomever you want!' she wanted to yell. 'I don't care!'

Sex was everywhere even when it wasn't. This was inevitable in a small asylum filled with feeling people, but the question of who you could do it with and in what context was the electric issue of the day, and it could make or break you. As the next chapter will show, the answer for clergy was just about to be underlined by the House of Bishops: only ever with your spouse of the opposite sex. This seemed completely mad from the perspective of the world beyond Cuddesdon's walls, in which sex before marriage had become normal, and remarriage after divorce the cause for a small party. In private, most at Cuddesdon agreed. But the pressure from the increasingly powerful conservative evangelical lobby was tightening its grip on the Church's major organs, and made even the liberals who ran Cuddesdon nervy.

Cuddesdon ordinands could just about get away with sex before marriage, so long as they kept it quiet. Remarriage was different. By the 1990s there were plenty of clergy who were willing to conduct marriages of divorcees, but no one could be ordained if he or she had remarried, or married a divorcee whose spouse was still alive. This caused some ordinands considerable distress. One of the luckier ones got an all-clear from a retired bishop who came to College at Easter to dispense homilies and confidential advice. 'I've fallen in love with a divorced man,' she told him, 'and he's asked me to marry him.' 'Is his wife alive?' the bishop asked anxiously. 'No,' the ordinand mumbled, 'she died from cancer last year.' 'Oh thank God for that!' he beamed.

Homosexuality (or 'homophilia' as the official church pronouncements liked to call it) was equally fraught. It was still all about men, rather than women. In the Anglo-Catholic tradition, being gay wasn't exactly *de rigueur*, but it was certainly more common than survey research would predict for the general population. The really spikey colleges like St Stephen's House in Oxford had cultures in which men called each other by girl's names like 'Doris' and 'Betty' and got excited about lacy cottas and embroidered chasubles. The scene is set by A. N. Wilson (who trained at Staggers), in his early novel, *Unguarded Hours*. A Dean opens the door of a student room to discover a threesome practising black magic. The participants are dispersed for a dose of real life. On their return, they exchange holiday reminiscences:

'Janie Jones went on the Industrial Relations course with Thelma and they found themselves a pair of absolutely smashing welders. Diana Dishman went to the Bin and had it off with a male nurse, so she's happy. Oh, and poor old Loony Lumsden went to the same Bin and they kept her there.'

'As a patient?'

'They didn't realise she was just visiting. Certified her at once. Must have been the Sarum cassock. So that's one good job done, having that very unattractive little person put behind bars.'

The only hint in all this that they are all men comes with the ambiguity of the term 'unattractive little person'.

Women were also a major problem at the time, not so much because of sex but because of their sex. Priests had always been male, and quite a lot wanted it to stay that way. In 1989 women could only be ordained as deacons, one rung down from a proper clergyperson, and the battle to allow them to be ordained as priests was in full swing. Linda was only the second full-time woman tutor to be appointed at Cuddesdon, and when the advert for her post in the *Church Times* called, in the small print, for someone with expertise in feminist theology, it was incendiary enough to elicit letters of protest to the College Principal. Janet Soskice had preceded, and there were two part-time female tutors as well, one of whom, Wendy Robinson, taught pastoral and counselling skills. The more liberal students loved Wendy because she kept confidences and brought a whiff of secular professionalism; the Anglo-Catholics despised her for the same reason.

The Anglo-Catholics at Cuddesdon were the most likely to be opposed to women's ordination, but they were generally more liberal about it than the 'traditionalist' Anglo-Catholics at St Stephen's House. For the latter, opposition had become almost the defining mark of their party. Some of the handful of women unwise enough to go to St Stephen's ended up being transferred to other colleges by compassionate DDOs, and the handful who stuck it out learnt to live with routine cruelties and humiliations. One year, at the end of their time in training, they sent the customary Petertide ordination cards to their brother students asking for their prayers, only to find them torn up into small pieces and returned to their own pigeonholes.

The other implacable opponents were conservative evangelicals. Traditionally opposed to Anglo-Catholics on almost everything, they were startled to find themselves on the same side of the argument over women's ordination, but were generally pragmatic enough to live with it, at least until the monstrous regiment of women was defeated. They used biblical texts to argue against change. Many insisted on the 'complementarity' of men and women, which seemed to boil down to the idea that women and children needed a man to make the really important decisions for them.

It was the liberals, well represented at Cuddesdon, who were the most willing of the clergy tribes to support women's ordination, though some still fought shy of a full-blooded support of gender equality, arguing that God had created women equal-but-different rather than equal-and-much-the-same. The newly founded Affirming Catholicism movement was supportive of women's ordination in deliberate distinction from the traditionalist Anglo-Catholics who insisted on the essentially and exclusively male nature of the priesthood. The latter were more worried about what ordaining women would do to dreams of union with Rome than about the lives of real women. They argued that the priest was an icon of Christ who, like the saviour and his disciples, was male (St Stephen's-style campness was compatible with this stance since it dispensed with the need for biological females altogether, excepting the Blessed Virgin Mary).

Where evangelicals still differed from the Anglo-Catholics was in their actual modes of clerical masculinity. They had long championed muscular rather than camp religion, and favoured philoprogenitivity over celibacy. They believed that real men have wives and children – lots of them (children, not wives). Evangelical manhood was played out through variations on the themes of responsible father-figure, successful businessman, heroic missionary, or evangelist. There were also scholarly variations, like the distinguished biblical scholar Dick France, Principal of Wycliffe Hall, whose support for the ordination of women was influential in changing evangelical opinion. (The more macho, shaven-headed, bearded, anti-gay kind of evangelical only appeared on the scene much later, once the evangelical battlefront shifted from women to gays.)

Training colleges were still a difficult place for women even when, as at Cuddesdon, the number of female ordinands was increasing. By 1989 the Church of England had been ruminating inconclusively over the 'woman question' for over a century; although women had always outnumbered men in the Church of England, they had existed as a sort of colonial population under the rule of a small clerical force. Their uprisings earlier in the century had been contained by simple means. In 1917, for example, Maude Royden, a campaigner for women's suffrage and ordination, was banned by the Principal from entering Cuddesdon when she arrived for a meeting of William Temple's Life and Liberty council (she resigned). But as women's equality gained ground, the Church's unthinking sexism and traditional exhortation to 'honour and obey' was becoming distinctly unpalatable to most of the population. Older generations of women remained in the pews, but their daughters abandoned them for alternative secular and spiritual options. In the process, what was being lost wasn't just generic 'bums on pews': it was the Anglican mothers, primary and secondary school teachers, nurses,

Sunday school teachers and health visitors who had kept the Church at the heart of English life.

There was only a glimmering of this unfolding disaster at Cuddesdon, partly because women's contribution to the Church was undervalued, and partly because supporters of women's ordination thought it would happen soon, and would rejuvenate the Church. In many ways it was the opponents of change who were most realistic. They knew just how long and hard the battle would rage, and they also knew that taking women seriously would cut to the quick of much that defined the Church and its clergy.

Despite feeble theological protests that God transcended gender, the reality was that the imagery of Father, Son, Judge, King and Lord shuttled through everything: liturgy, hymns, Bible, structures. Much of the Church's ethical teaching was similarly biased. Change was going to require a radical re-examination of the whole piece – from God to the toilets. The work was already underway in the USA, where books like Mary Daly's *Beyond God the Father* and Sallie McFague's *Models of God* challenged Christian theology, and Starhawk's *The Spiral Dance* and Rosemary Radford Ruether's *Women-Church* empowered women to create rituals on their own terms. By the 1980s even the Church of England was starting to produce feminist theology and liturgies.

The St Hilda Community was founded in 1987 as a body which tried to model a form of cooperation between men and women in liturgy, which used inclusive language, and which invited ordained women from other countries to come and celebrate openly, rather than, as was usual at the time, clandestinely. Despite being chased out of Anglican premises by the then bishop of London, Graham

Leonard, the community was a seedbed for new liturgical resources, and collects like the following by Janet Morley were starting to be used by the more radical staff and students at Cuddesdon:

God our mother,

you hold our life within you,

nourish us at your breast,

and teach us to walk alone.

Help us to receive your tenderness

and respond to your challenge

that others may draw life from us,

in your name.

Amen.

Comforted by such sentiments, the women at Cuddesdon continued to hope for change. Many campaigned for it as part of MOW, the Movement for the Ordination of Women, and a good number of their male peers supported them. But there were no brownie badges to be gained by being a feminist in Cuddesdon, and it was wrenchingly difficult to combine the virtues of gentle and self-sacrificial Christian womanhood with the angry determination of a campaigner against one's own subjection.

The real prizes in the Church at the time weren't being awarded to those who fought for women's rights, but to those who fought for 'the poor'. This wasn't new. It was part of the Church of England's long-standing commitment to works of charity and benevolence, which had evolved from support for the rural poor to concern for the casualties of a growing industrial society. It had taken shape in the nineteenth century in things like missions to inner cities, and in the mid-twentieth it fuelled the Church's support for the welfare state. The *Faith in the City* report commissioned by Archbishop Robert Runcie and published in 1985 gave it a new lease of life by adding a sharp critique of Thatcherite policies.

*Faith in the City*'s practical outcomes – besides irritating people like Charles Moore and John Selwyn Gummer – were the establishment of the Church Urban Fund to support projects in deprived areas, and a renewed emphasis on the importance of clergy 'getting alongside the poor'. A spell in a UPA (Urban Priority Area) became a very sound move for clergy hoping to attain higher office. Cuddesdon took this so seriously that it had appointed one of *Faith in the City*'s authors as Vice Principal, and purchased a council house in Sheffield where ordinands were sent for short spells to get alongside the poor. A link had also been forged with the 'Urban Theology Unit', where John Vincent and his team offered crash courses in a Christianized version of class war. The aim was not to help the poor, but to learn from them. The inspiration was Liberation Theology, which held that only the oppressed could appreciate the radicalism of Jesus and read the Bible properly, because the rich were blinkered by their privilege. Theology was therefore to be done in 'base communities' where the working class – 'the poor' – would do the theology and the privileged rich would get alongside them and repent.

There were a number of problems with this. One was that working-class people in Sheffield didn't seem as keen as the poor in Latin America to join a base community, or to be got alongside. Another was that anyone hailing from Cuddesdon was cast by the

Urban Theology Unit in the role of oppressor, while all those in inner-city Sheffield were counted as fearless conscience-raisers and/ or oppressed working classes. This struck even the most naturally guilt-ridden as both batty and condescending. There were quite a few students at Cuddesdon from working-class backgrounds, and even those who had made it to university didn't necessarily feel they'd graduated with a degree in heartless oppression of the proletariat. The few genuine public schoolboys tended to take it on the chin, while everyone else either got cross, or treated it as an acceptable escape from the equally wacky world of Cuddesdon.

Left-wing politics was the one thing which seemed to unite all the training colleges and the clergy they turned out, whatever their churchmanship. It was absolutely essential in order to 'get on', and those who didn't have leftish sentiments tended to keep jolly quiet. This was a legacy of the Church's entanglement with the post-war ethos, and it set the clergy at odds with the majority of Anglicans who were more right-leaning and Conservative-voting than the population as whole. Clerical socialism was reinforced by the clergy's own brand of welfare dependency: from the moment they were accepted for training, everything was paid for, as if by a benevolent paymaster in the sky. 'Enterprise' was a dirty word.

Thatcherism didn't entirely bypass Cuddesdon. There was a sharp increase in the number and quality of cars in the College car park, and the Principal – who was engaged in a fundraising drive for a new building – took to telling everyone that 'money is the sacrament of seriousness'. But the monetarist revolution made no serious impact. In the 1987 election there were probably no more than four or five members of the entire community at Cuddesdon who voted Conservative, and they only confessed much later. Hatred of Mrs Thatcher was simply a given.

The other well-intentioned attempt to mitigate the experience of being shut away in a theological college, and keep up with the times, was the 'Coventry experience'. Whereas the 'Sheffield experience' was intended to raise awareness of poverty, the Coventry experience was to raise awareness of multiculturalism and, in particular, of multi-faith Britain. The project was in many ways more sensible because, whereas industrial Britain was disappearing fast, multicultural Britain was on the rise. It was also more challenging for an English church with an imperial, not to say racist, past.

The Coventry experience was much briefer than the Sheffield one. Students were billeted for a few days with families 'of other faiths'. Linda was sent with a female ordinand to a Muslim family who put them in one of their spare terrace houses where everything – from beds to sofas – was covered in creaky plastic covers. They ate with the other women of the extended family in a strictly gender-segregated regime, and were fed largely on rice and carrots. While this was monotonous, it was preferable to the fizzy tuna served to the male ordinands billeted next door. In the daytime there were visits to different places of worship – temple, Gurdwara and mosque – and talks with some of their members. Many were thoughtful and impressive, but one more opportunistic imam decided to lecture for well over an hour on why Islam surpassed Christianity in every respect. Being Church of England, everyone was too polite to disagree.

Yet Cuddesdon was not without its virtues. There were truly good and impressive people there, both staff and students, some of whom really could have pursued more lucrative careers elsewhere. There was still a huge amount of idealism. People dedicated themselves to the Church because they believed in God, and wanted to make a difference. The benevolent presence and occasional visits of Robert Runcie, a former Principal, smiled down on the place. Church reports like *The Church and the Bomb* and *Faith in the City* made clergy in training feel that the Church was still a major player in society, and that it could say and do things that mattered. They weren't yet angry bystanders throwing rocks at wider society, because they still felt integral to things: the established church was there for everyone, and so were they.

This confidence spread through the theology and spirituality of the place. The academic training was serious, and students took the Theology degree at Oxford as well as other qualifications. There was no anti-intellectualism, and no one thought that the pursuit of learning and truth had nothing to do with God. The spiritual life was rigorous, with matins and evensong every day, regular communion, and compline for those who wanted it. True, there was a fair bit of spiritual competition around, with people vying to outdo one another in piety, but most left Cuddesdon knowing how to conduct worship well, and with the scaffolding of a personal spiritual discipline.

'We knew there were problems,' said Mike Hampson, a student of the time, 'but renewal was in the air. Morale was high throughout the institution. It seemed that everything was in place for the Church of England to become the soul of the nation for the next generation, as it had been for generations before. In reality the dead weight of its history would continue to drag the institution down ever further into its hopeless spiral of decline. I walked away 13 years later. Half of my college contemporaries had already left.'

Like so much of the Church, Cuddesdon's weakness was its complacent sense of entitlement and its failure to grasp what was happening in society. There was an inability to accept that the post-war settlement was over and that the Church, like other institutions, would have to change. Somehow it was assumed that it was a glorious exception, which God could not possibly allow to fail.

The atmosphere of a gentleman's club whose day is over, but which can't quite see it, struck many visitors. The social sciences were the one subject which never appeared on the curriculum at Cuddesdon and most other Anglican training colleges, which meant that the study of contemporary religion and social change was off the menu. The Church of England never dreamt of doing research about itself, and was unwilling to allow others to do so. It did not consider comparing itself to other Protestant churches or taking advice from outsiders. It was happy to study its past but not its present, and eager to pronounce about society but not to take a hard look at the evidence.

This was short-sighted at best, arrogant at worst. Clerical parties and the battles between them were beginning to seem more interesting and absorbing than anything outside, and the world was being squinted at through a narrow lens. Controversies over sex, gender and the family were starting to take over and blot out – or keep out – what was happening in the world.

Like the wider Church, Cuddesdon's weak spot was honest self-appraisal. It enjoyed the view from the top of its pretty Oxfordshire hill looking out, but had no interest in looking back.

# 3

# Gays and evangelicals

For almost all of the twentieth century the evangelical tradition in the Church of England was that of the public school officer class. There were of course plenty of working-class evangelicals but they tended to be dissenters or non-conformists of various sorts. Within the Church of England the conservative evangelicals formed an entirely recognizable clan, who had all been to the same schools, the same summer camps, and the same universities. Their leading figure throughout the 1960s and 1970s was John Stott, the Rector Emeritus of All Souls, Langham Place. When he died in 2011 he was probably the single most revered figure in the global white evangelical scene after Billy Graham. His obituaries described him as 'The evangelical Pope'. His books sold in millions. He was credited with keeping the evangelical presence in the Church of England alive in the 1960s, resisting a more full-blooded fundamentalism, and in the 1970s with turning the whole Anglo-American evangelical movement towards social action and a commitment to the third world.

The organization he left behind him is quite astonishingly rich; the one church at Langham Place employs twenty-seven people: his foundation raises millions of dollars in North America. Yet his life and career illustrates the extraordinary introversion of the evangelical movement in the Church of England, not least because he is regarded by his followers as a man who turned them outwards. For all the energy of their attempts at conversion, there's no evidence that his style of Anglicanism ever broke free from its core constituencies: the English upper-middle classes and the universities they attend.

Stott's brand of evangelical preaching was absolutely clear, authoritative, and desperately anti-emotional. In part this was a military virtue: the traditional stoicism of the English officer classes. Stott, the son of a Harley Street doctor, had been socialized in this fashion himself: sent to board at prep school aged eight, and then at thirteen to Rugby, the school of Harry Flashman and of Dr Arnold. The tradition of evangelical piety at Rugby ran deep. One biographer reckoned that in his day Stott would have had to attend thirteen Prayer Book services every single week. He was also beaten, of course, as everyone was, but he rose through the brutal and unforgiving hierarchies that the boys built for themselves to become Head Boy. No wonder he emerged from this convinced that those who did not give their lives to Jesus would be damned forever. Although he became a pacifist at Cambridge, he never lost his belief in order and in hierarchy, nor in the place of Christian gentlemen therein.

In a sermon from the late 1960s he urged his parishioners to consider: 'If we have domestic servants, do we treat them as human beings to be considered or as underlings to be bossed around? How do we run our businesses and care for our employees? If we are landlords, what do our tenants think of our Christianity? Are we considerate and courteous to the assistants from whom we buy in the shops?'

His energy and powers of leadership are attested by the fact that by 1957 he had managed to commission 317 parish workers to work the doorsteps of his parish. His honesty was troubled by the fact that the working classes still stayed away. By the 1960s he had come to believe that only God could convert the whole of England. In the meantime, the social and sexual conservatism of the movement cut it off more and more from the society around it. This exclusion fed the conviction that society needed their example more than ever, and that, in turn, strengthened society's determination that it did not.

Stott is significant in this story partly because he was the last evangelical leader to believe whole-heartedly in an established national church. That is to say, he believed that everyone in England ought to be a Christian, which meant, to him, a Calvinist, and that the Church of England was the organization which could bring about this happy state. Such an understanding of Christianity – and of England – was in its way quite as far out of touch as the bishops in St George's House but the evangelicals were much quicker to grasp the organizational consequences of this failure than were their liberal enemies. Perhaps this is because Calvinists always have in reserve an archetypal understanding of Christians as a beleaguered minority – a faithful remnant. Where whole countries are supposed to be Calvinist, as Puritan England was, they have to be surrounded by treacherous and powerful neighbours from whom God will deliver them; but congregations, too, can form islands or beacons of virtue in a godless society. So the transformation from a social to a congregational church does not violate the emotional grammar of Calvinism in the same way that it can for more outward-facing styles of Christianity.

In fact Stott's style of Christianity had become almost completely congregational even as it thought of itself as societal. The society of which it felt it was a part looked more and more like a fiction. Appeals to a vanishing moral code might be cast as appeals to an intellectual authority, but they had and have no force unless they are also appeals to habits of behaviour and of mind. One example is the fact that Stott's Christianity found it deeply uplifting to believe that Christ was tortured to death because we all deserve that punishment, and that the Father's justice is demonstrated by the way that he accepted this suffering from his Son instead of exacting it from us. In fact faith in this doctrine (technically known as 'penal substitutionary atonement') is considered by evangelicals one of the distinguishing marks of a real Christian. Yet unless you have spent your adolescence lonely, beaten, and constantly preached at from the Prayer Book, or otherwise abused, it doesn't make much sense. In fact the doctrine compels some victims into revolt: the god of Rugby school in Stott's time is also the god of Christopher Hitchens and Richard Dawkins.

In their struggles against the breakdown of patriarchal authority, the conservative evangelicals resisted feminism, resisted divorce, and anathematized homosexuality. All did enormous damage to the Church of England, and though the last may have been the least important to them it was fundamental to the collapse which this book charts. When we consider the great evangelical revolt over homosexuality it is important to remember that evangelicals, like other fervent Christians, were disproportionately likely to be gay. The reasons for this remain an interesting mystery. Colin Haycraft, the atheist husband of the fervently reactionary Catholic writer Alice Thomas Ellis, used to say that 'religion is for women and queers' but that doesn't answer the question. In societies where religion is taken for granted as part of the fabric of life, the overwhelming majority of believers, like the society around them, will be straight. But even then, there will be a particular attraction to the profession of religion among gay people. In part this must be because religious professionals are respected for celibacy. It may also be because religious faith deals with fundamental questions of identity, both collective and individual. These must specially trouble anyone growing up who realizes that there is something unusual about their sexual orientation.

In the Church of England the matter of male homosexuality had a further twist. Among the imperial classes, it had been customary for 150 years for their sons to be educated in single-sex boarding schools where opportunistic sexual predation was a constant possibility. So the ideas of decency, purity and cleanliness, which were in any case central to dealing with sex, might take on a particularly homophobic tinge where adolescent sexual rumblings were concerned. At Marlborough, a school founded for sons of the clergy, sexual aggression was part of the normal repertoire of bullying at least until the early 1970s. Unpopular boys would be hunted down and have their genitals ritually smeared with boot polish. Really unpopular ones could be gang-raped anally with a broomstick. It was a part of the character-building process. For anyone who was in their heart uninterested in women the spectacle must have been a peculiarly horrible one, suggesting that no loving sexual relationship between men or even between boys could ever be possible. And even where such open brutalities were unknown, the homoerotic element of male friendship was sentimentalized into something impossible.

*The Returns of Love*, a slim book published pseudonymously in 1970, highlighted the torments of being a celibate gay evangelical minister. To understand the poisonous knots into which the church would tie itself, it is worth remembering that the book was unpalatably liberal for its time. *The Returns of Love* is very distressing to read.

The author, who calls himself 'Alex Davidson', is absolutely clear about his sexual identity. He has read Kinsey. He knows there are some homosexuals who are also attracted to women and he is certain that he is not one of them. In his own jargon, he is an invert, not a pervert.

Perhaps the single most cringe-making section of the book recounts his efforts to settle for a woman as his wife. He finds a candidate without any apparent problem.

She is a convinced Christian with a living faith, we can talk about the things of God together and pray together, and we complement each other in our understanding of the gospel, hers being feminine and intuitive and mine masculine and logical ... we have similar interests ... we do in fact feel at home in each other's company, relaxed, free from the tensions which can arise from a difference either in background or in character. So far so good ... But ... No woman has ever attracted me physically, so why should this one? Oh, I persevere with the relationship, hoping that one day the obvious may dawn even on my dim sight ... And then I go home and cry myself to sleep.

The book is written in the form of letters to 'Peter', a close Christian friend with whom 'Davidson' is, as he confesses, helplessly in love. Although they have known each other, we learn, for ten years as increasingly close friends, it is only as a result of his own tortured confession that he realizes that Peter, too, is a homosexual. This is followed by a second, almost more terrible shock: Peter doesn't fancy 'Davidson' at all. He just wants to remain friends.

That's just as well, because 'Davidson's' first reaction to the discovery that he is in love with another gay man is to decide they must never meet again. Once he realizes he is safe from sex, he continues the friendship. But his yearnings remain and run into an extraordinary and revealing passage of self-hatred:

I suppose one who had the gift would be able to turn my catalogue into a poem, a love-lyric in praise of the beloved. Not of Mary, alas – poor Mary – but of that other with whom I feel myself to be in harmony not only spiritually, intellectually, socially, and psychologically, but physically and emotionally as well. O Peter, Peter … If I loved Mary as I love you, I should have proposed to her, refused to take no for an answer from her, and been engaged to be married to her, long before this.

Already I hate myself for writing all that. I have taken too much advantage of the offer of a listening ear which you made to me so long ago. I have tried to be restrained and objective, but with little success, I'm afraid. I know your own experience of homosexual attraction has not had this colouring of sentimentality; so although you are a man of your word, and will therefore still be reading, I realize that what you are reading must be distasteful to you in the extreme, pages of nauseating slop. And, as I say, I hate myself for it. On the surface it may not seem so evil a thing as an outright physical involvement would be; but sin is sin, and this emotional involvement is sinful, just as that is.

These are not the words of a man who hates himself for being gay – they are the words of a man who hates himself for having feelings at all. His deepest emotions, he thinks, must be 'distasteful to you in the extreme, pages of nauseating slop'. Only a sense of duty could compel his friend to read them.

This is the morbid swelling of the Calvinist ego, inflamed and agonizing. But it is almost as bad for the people around him: the hapless 'Mary', whom he has led on in a trial of his feelings; even Peter, the friend who is the recipient of these confidences, and is told he's not nearly as great a sinner, or at least as indecent a man, as 'Davidson', since his gay sexual experiences (and he has had them) had no feeling in them nor connection with love.

The peculiar combination of self-abasement and self-esteem in these letters – of cringing coupled with immense pride at knowing that he ought to cringe – goes to the heart of the public school evangelical. It places the Christian disciple plainly in the lower, and hellish reaches of an exclusive and purportedly heavenly school. He is at the same time a worm desperately seeking for rules to obey and a kind of aristocrat profoundly conscious of his superiority to the lesser breeds who don't understand that there is a law at all.

'Give me the magnetic needle that says "This is North"', he writes, 'or the law of gravity that says "This is Down", and then I know where I am. Show me the scripture that says "This is Sin", and then I know where I am; and though the temptation to the sin in question may tear my heart in two, by the grace of God I will not transgress that law.'

But for liberals, people who accept and even love the 'nauseating slop' they find in their own hearts, he has nothing but scorn. They are

> mere hirelings ... who therefore have no compunction about contradicting the Shepherd and saying that the answer is to abandon the old paths of righteousness in favour of some new morality. In practical terms, all that their 'pastoral care' amounts to is a cynical agreement with Oscar Wilde, that the only way to get rid of a temptation is to yield to it. But I don't want that kind of care. I delight in the law of God after the inward man, and I don't want them to accept and condone my sin.

Something has changed profoundly and for the better since those words were written. This kind of self-flagellation no longer appears as a mark of virtue. It is something wrong in itself, whether or not poor 'Davidson' should have given in to his urges. What he's denying himself is not so much sex as love, understanding, and even forgiveness.

One of the many kinds of pride that an elite education instils is a confidence that you can think through any problem that defeats your inferiors. But in 'Davidson's' tortured discussion of whether sodomy might be forgiven if it were ennobled by love it is perfectly obvious that he is working entirely from first principles with no practical experience at all of the situations he so clearly analyses. For a comparable spectacle of intellectual arrogance, you'd have to skip forward thirty years to Rowan Williams lecturing the nation on economics or Sharia law.

In retrospect, the end of National Service sounded the death knell for the public school evangelical project, which was itself a kind of ideal of national service. The ideal of a unified, hierarchical society, in which everyone had their station and their duty, was not ignoble, though it was often dreadfully unjust. But it had been justified by centuries of ultimately successful wars. After Suez, that could no longer be an organizing principle of British society. The peacetime welfare state was not just a consummation of the Church of England's vision of society, but one which made the Church's continuation in the old forms quite impossible, not least because it gradually elevated some women into positions of leadership over men. The rebellion that 'Alex Davidson' tried to quell in his heart was spreading through all of English society. For the most part it was entirely successful. Only where gay people were concerned did the conservatives mount an apparently successful defence of the old hierarchy. It was strange ground to fight on, and it would be disastrous for the Church of England.

There is a curious paradox here. Homosexuality isn't one thing. It's certainly not just a listing of things men do with their willies. What is involved is a tangle of affection, temperament and imagination, all held within a net of social relationships. Sexuality can express and enact a great many emotions: dominance and submission quite as much as tenderness, contempt as much as trust. Boys who were as profoundly gay as 'Davidson' and had no attraction at all to women were much more likely to be repelled by the whole business than the cheery buggers who simply wanted an outlet for hormonal exuberance. One of the first gay priests Andrew met in the 1980s was a middle-aged man who had been brought up very pious and protected and still remembered the shock when he was doing his national service and the drill sergeant announced that he would 'fuck his orders into your ear'.

In the Anglo-Catholic tradition there was considerable tolerance, later enthusiastic sympathy, for gay men, but this was all understood as something which must be kept from the public. After the scandal at St Stephen's House of which A.N. Wilson's novel was a fictional shadow, an earnest man named David Hope was put in to clean the place up. He clamped down on the camp to such effect that his students nicknamed him Ena the Cruel after Ena Sharples in *Coronation Street*, but he was not hostile to gay people as such. One of his ordinands, a shy Welsh boy who, like Hope, took the Catholic Church very seriously, came to him in the mid-1970s to say he had fallen in love, expecting to be expelled. 'To my astonishment, he congratulated me', the young man wrote, twenty-seven years later, still with the same partner. 'He told me I had been a miserable, introverted academic, and that this relationship would make me a better human being and a better priest. He was right; it did.'

Jeffrey John, who told this story, had known he was gay since his mid-teens, and had once asked his GP if there was any cure. Because medical records had to be disclosed, this was known to the Church's selection board for ministry, which sent him for a psychiatric assessment before he could be accepted at a theological college.

It was not just the gay men who dealt with their sexuality by ignoring it, however obvious it might be. Public school homosexuality of 'Davidson's' sort belonged within the same social order as pipe-smoking bishops, and both depended on a society in which emotion was understood as shaming and intimacy as a threat. That tradition persisted for a long time among public school Calvinists. John Stott's successor as Rector of All Souls, Richard Bewes, once gave communion to the Evangelical Group on General Synod, and when he came to the Peace, when members of the congregation are exhorted to shake hands, or even to embrace their neighbours, he stood very upright and said that since they were all brothers and sisters together, who knew each other's fellowship, there was no need for anything more than a manly punch on the shoulder.

Stott's greatest achievement in English church politics had come in the mid-1960s, when he safeguarded the place of conservative evangelicalism, minus American fundamentalism's distrust of the state and elite society, within the Church of England. His only rival at that time as a leader of English Calvinism was Martyn Lloyd-Jones, the minister at Westminster Chapel, and in 1966 the two men clashed over whether Calvinist evangelicals of their sort should leave the Church of England because it was riddled with sin and liberalism. Evangelicals, wrote Lloyd-Jones, should not be 'mixed up with infidels and sceptics and deniers of the truth'. Those who did not follow him had 'bowed the knee to Baal'.

But Stott won the contest. He was careful to maintain that he was a Christian first, an evangelical second, and finally, if tenuously, an Anglican. But an Anglican he remained, and he urged his followers to do likewise. This appeared to the hardliners as a triumph of sociology over theology, but in practice it could work the other way: young fundamentalists who had no experience of the Church of England could enter it in the belief that it shared their theology.

One beneficiary of this policy was Tony Higton, who had learnt his Christianity in the early 1960s, growing up among the Plymouth Brethren in a Derbyshire village; the first Anglican service he attended was at Stott's church, All Souls, Langham Place.

While the rest of the Church was struggling to come to terms with the changes in society after about 1965, Higton came from a tradition which might have been more at home in about 1665. To him the Church of England was still a Puritan body, bound by the law of England to the supremacy of Scripture. The theological college he attended, Oak Hill, paid no attention to denominational boundaries: although he became an Anglican while he was a student there, he seems to have been educated in complete ignorance of any other kind of Anglicanism than the Calvinist evangelical tradition.

By 1976, he had his first parish, Hawkwell, in the unfashionable Thatcherite end of south Essex. Already, as he wrote in an autobiography, he was wrestling with the devil:

By the end of 1976, 24 people had professed faith in Christ. But a strange thing also happened. It was just amazing how many problems erupted at about 6 pm on Thursdays. The rest of the week seemed relatively problem free, but not Thursday evening. Team members felt ill – just for a few hours, sometimes only until they were visiting the first home for the evening. Children became ill. Car problems developed. One member reversed into a passing car. Even someone as hesitant as me about demons and spiritual warfare eventually had to admit there was something more than coincidence here.

He reordered the church buildings, introduced charismatic worship with weeping, prophecy and choruses instead of hymns, and demanded that the congregation tithe. Later they moved into exorcisms as well. He was, in all but name and pension fund, an independent puritan. His congregation split in 1979. He wrote:

> From a personal point of view I was very sad to see these people leave. If only the wrong attitudes could have gone, not the people. But since the people consistently refused to repent, the Lord had to remove them along with their attitudes. It was vital that such attitudes should not remain in the church, otherwise it would be severely hindered in its work and witness.

It is difficult to imagine any form of Christianity more different in tone and ambition from the measured, courteous and scholarly concerns of Windsor Castle and of Cuddesdon, where everyone took for granted that the Church existed, in the words of William Temple, for the benefit of those who were not its members.

The two worlds were to collide violently, with consequences that shape the story told here.

Higton first tried to move on to the national stage in 1984, when David Jenkins was consecrated bishop of Durham. He raised £2,000 from his congregation to write to every clergyman in Britain denouncing the confusions of the Church. What he particularly objected to was the idea that you could be a Christian, as David Jenkins claimed, without believing in either the bodily resurrection or the Virgin Birth. To the Calvinist mind it was perfectly obvious that people who did not believe in these things were not Christians, and were going to hell.

There was also a second-order problem with liberalism, from Higton's point of view: bishops who themselves believed in the literal resurrection and Virgin Birth could still be false prophets if they tolerated those Christians or clergy who did not.

That is why he mounted the campaign against David Jenkins, and John Habgood, who had consecrated him. But of course that campaign was a resounding failure. For the liberals, and for anyone who believed in the Church as a part of English culture, Jenkins became a beacon in the darkness. He got people talking about Christianity in pubs and workplaces and this seemed to them to reaffirm it as a part of society.

So Higton, by now elected to the General Synod, found another means of attacking the liberals: homosexuality. It is not clear whether this was originally his idea or that of the most prominent Calvinist politician on the Synod, David Holloway. Holloway was the vicar of Jesmond, a district of Newcastle where he had a flourishing student congregation – the strongest base of evangelicalism has always been its churches for students, which were fed by Christian Unions in universities, and were to be found in every university town.

Holloway was a man of inexhaustible energy, always ready with a scheme or a sermon. He was convinced throughout his long career in ecclesiastical politics that God wanted him to be a church leader, but which church God wanted him to lead, and how God wanted it led, were questions on which his mind changed with his fortunes.

In the mid-1980s, when Higton was elected to the General Synod, Holloway had reached the summit of his power there. He sat on the standing committee, the group of six who controlled, as much as anyone did, the agenda and direction of the Synod, and he wrote and argued passionately in favour of a church where all authority was concentrated in the Synod, and the bishops did its bidding. We'll never know how his views would have changed had he become a bishop, since providence had other ideas.

In any case, Holloway was quick to grasp that Higton's cause would be best advanced by an attack on 'the gays'. He explained all this to Andrew, and to Clifford Longley of *The Times*, in a subterranean Westminster wine bar in the autumn of 1987. He wanted the journalists to know he was a sophisticate. He had nothing personal against the gays. What mattered was that the liberals were vulnerable on the question.

By that autumn, Higton's Private Member's motion had acquired an unstoppable momentum. It was entirely unambiguous:

This Synod reaffirms the biblical standard, given for the well-being of society:

1. that sexual intercourse should take place only between a man and a woman who are married to each other;

2. that fornication, adultery and homosexual acts are sinful in all circumstances;

3. that Christian leaders are called to be exemplary in all spheres of morality, including sexual morality, as a condition of being appointed to or remaining in office.

And calls upon the church to show Christ-like compassion to those who have fallen into sexual sin, encouraging them to repent and receive absolution, and offering the ministry of healing to all who suffer physically or emotionally as a result of such sin.

No one believed there was any chance that the General Synod would pass such a motion. Bishops might lack a clear understanding of how the outside world might see them, but even the most self-righteous among them recoiled from proclaiming themselves 'exemplary in all spheres of morality'. Nor did they want to drive out the gays: they just wanted them to go away. Higton thought of himself as a prophet, summoned by God to reprove and correct the Church of England. But the Synod was not a body for prophets.

In fact, it's a little hard to say what exactly the Synod was for at all. The causes of the Synod's existence are easy to explain, but its purpose remained mysterious. From the point of view of its inventors it was enough that the Synod should exist. That it should do something, or accomplish anything, was a novelty which the Church had not yet received.

The brief answer is that the Synod was invented to resolve the difficulties that arose once the Church of England was no longer the religion of the English state in a straightforward sense. The separation had been plain to lawyers since 1917, when a court judgment stated clearly that the law of England was not Christian. That made it hard to justify the situation in which the Church was governed by Parliamentary legislation. This theoretical problem became acute and practical in 1928, when the evangelical party in the House of Commons rejected a Prayer Book revision that the Church had prepared on the grounds that it was too Catholic.

That particular form of evangelical lay revolt via Parliament persisted until the 1960s, but by 1965 the lay evangelical party in the Commons was an etiolated anachronism. Protestantism was no longer a part of English identity as it had been for the preceding 400 years. The bigotry of Ian Paisley Sr, which would have been entirely unremarkable in 1914, suddenly looked repulsive and foreign to the English, even though Paisley's view of Rome, and of the Pope as the Antichrist, had been in the mainstream of Anglican evangelical discourse for centuries.

By the early twentieth century it had become clear that Parliament as a whole had lost its appetite for regulating the Church of England. The solution, which appeared in 1919, was a form of partial disestablishment. A new body, the Church Assembly (reconstituted in 1970 as the General Synod), would have the power to formulate church legislation that would then be submitted to Parliament. The bishops didn't trust laypeople to use power responsibly, and fought successfully against the idea of giving them a vote. They proposed instead an arcane system which would give a semblance of democracy while allowing them to retain power. As Major Harry Barnes MP, speaking at the second reading of the Enabling Bill of the Church Assembly in 1919, said, 'The fact that the organisation proposed by the Archbishop of Canterbury is precisely the same organisation as has been adopted by Lenin is attributable to the desire of both to secure the same end ... The real principle at the root of Bolshevism is a desire to combine a democratic form with autocratic effects, and that is what has taken place in this Constitution.'

So the Synod was not a democratic body and the House of Laity did not represent democratic or lay governance in the way that Parliament had done. But it placed the power struggles between contending clerical oligarchies, whether donnish or Calvinist, on a new stage, and loosened the connection with common sense.

The phrase used to describe this system was that the Church was 'episcopally led but synodically governed', which was understood by the bishops to mean that the function of the Synod was to endorse their decisions, but by the more enthusiastic members of the Synod to mean that they could teach the bishops real Christianity, and by the permanent civil servants of the Synod to mean that they ran everything.

In its first decade the Synod was largely concerned with the terms and conditions of clergy, and with liturgical revisions of the sort which had caused so much controversy in 1928. The result was a new confusion of services which replaced the old unifying framework of the Prayer Book. In its second decade, the 1980s, the Synod began to be concerned with other matters. The main struggle was over women priests.

By this time, the Synod was run by an introverted bureaucracy under a former treasury civil servant, Derek Pattinson. Pattinson himself was gay, but not at the time ostentatiously so. He worked, sometimes with and sometimes against, the bishops, to manipulate the agenda and control the various committees on which the evangelicals and Catholics fought with unremitting energy over trivial matters.

The Synod itself was composed of three sections, or 'Houses', all of which had to agree to any controversial legislation. Diocesan bishops sat there as of right. Suffragans (lesser bishops) might be elected to the House of Bishops. The House of Clergy was filled by election from among their peers; the House of Laity, by election from the members of deanery synods, a kind of committee once defined as a roomful of Anglicans all wishing they were somewhere else. The system worked fairly well for bishops and clergy in as much as both groups represented more or less the opinion among their electorate. But among the laity it was a gift for activists and a recipe for entryism. The greater part of the Anglican laity don't even go to church, let alone to church committees, so their views are only by accident represented on the Synod.

Conservative evangelicals were the first to understand and later ruthlessly to exploit the fact that the only real qualification for election to the General Synod was wanting to be elected there. They were far better organized than liberals, and their leaders were happy to issue clear commands with a realistic expectation of being obeyed.

The bishops and the secretariat of the Synod had done their best to keep the Higton motion from being debated. But the rules said that those motions with the greatest number of signatures must be debated, and Higton's had gained more, more quickly, than any other in the history of the Synod. In the summer of 1987 he claimed there were twenty priests with Aids in the Church. By the autumn of 1987 a debate had become unavoidable.

It would not have been so poisonous but for the political atmosphere of the time. In the aftermath of *Faith in the City* the Thatcherites were out to get the Church of England. This was partly for cultural and economic reasons: the Church was the British institution which most completely expressed One Nation conservatism and this was something the Thatcherites were determined to stamp out. But there was also a faction which saw in Parliament an ally against women priests. Graham Leonard, the bishop of London, had a heavy-drinking and hard-of-hearing press spokesman, a former naval officer named Norman Hood, who was a tireless intriguer. He was involved at one stage in a plot to buy the *Church Times* with Jeffrey Archer's money and turn it into a campaigning organ against women priests. In the context of church politics at the time this seemed a perfectly reasonable ambition.

These opportunistic theological conservatives were entirely unbothered by homosexuality but determined to destroy the grip that Runcie and Habgood had on the Church. So from the *Telegraph* to the *Sun* the conservative press was agitating against the Church as the Higton vote approached. Odder and nastier things happened. One high camp London church was burned down in an arson attack and another was attacked. It was the time of Aids hysteria. The previous year the diocese of London had started to draw up plans for the epidemic. The bishop, Graham Leonard, had told Malcolm Johnson, the rector of St Botolph's, that there were around two hundred gay clergy under his care. Three had the virus already and the younger ones were not being, in the bishop's words, 'careful'. But none of this could possibly be discussed in public.

When they saw the Higton amendment rising like the Kraken from the depths of the House of Laity the bishops just ran for the hills. They put up Michael Baughen, a former team vicar and then rector at Stott's church, who was now the bishop of Chester, to modify and slightly soften the text.

Forty-five members voted for a wrecking amendment put forward by Malcolm Johnson. After that was lost almost everyone in Synod voted for the modified Higton amendment. Those bishops who disagreed with it took the view that it had no power to bind them. That was certainly the view of David Jenkins, watching a portion of the debate from the press gallery with Andrew. Like Ronnie Bowlby, the old Etonian bishop of Southwark, he had a policy of ordaining gay men only if he was satisfied they were in stable relationships.

They were wrong. In retrospect, the Higton motion (as it became known) marked a turning point for the Church of England, and a step on the road to self-destruction. It was a major defeat for the liberals: a conservative evangelical salient that they were never able entirely to pinch off or to pass around. The bishops would find it harder and harder to evade it, especially as a major aim of evangelical policy was to ensure there would be no more bishops like David Jenkins, ever. It established the ground for decades of trench warfare. And it was very shortly followed by a scandal that went off with the force of one of those titanic mines which could annihilate whole sections of the Western Front.

In the autumn of 1987, Church House Publishing produced its biennial directory of the serving clergy, *Crockford's*, complete with an anonymous preface surveying the ecclesiastical scene: not, one would have thought, a matter for immediate suicide. But within four days of publication, the author was dead, and reading what he wrote it is possible to understand why. The central paragraphs of the preface, the hinge on which the whole argument turned, contained a lucid and bitterly cruel portrait of the Archbishop of Canterbury, Robert Runcie, as a scheming vacillator who would destroy the Church of England as it had existed for centuries, not from malice so much as from a profound aversion to its founding principles. The mechanism of this destruction would be the introduction of women priests. Such charges might be the small change of ecclesiastical politics, but to the unbelieving world it seemed remarkable that the Church should sponsor an anonymous attack of such memorable venom on its own leadership.

Anonymity did not survive long. Some priests and (mostly Tory) MPs crowded forward to put their names to the criticisms made: indeed, the phrase most often quoted, that Dr Runcie 'was usually found nailing his colours to the fence', was actually due to Frank Field. The story was serious, front-page news for days. In the general excitement, the author could not remain concealed. His style, lapidary and savage, like an obsidian knife, was immediately recognizable.

Runcie had recognized the arguments of the preface at once, since they stemmed from a friend of his, Gary Bennett, an Oxford historian and synodical politician who had just been elevated to the Crown Appointments Commission, the committee which chose candidates for bishoprics, whose names went forward to the Prime Minister for selection. Within twenty-four hours of the preface's appearing, Bennett had denied he was the author to at least half a dozen journalists and worked himself into a very difficult position.

His difficulties were compounded by one unmentionable fact. He was gay, as was the man who had commissioned the preface, the Secretary General of the General Synod, Derek Pattinson. It had already been an autumn to excite the conspiratorial and persecuted tendencies of Anglican gays. The tabloid headlines reporting the Higton debate had taken the view that it was a triumph for the gay clergy, who would not now be driven from the Church as Higton had intended. 'Runcie says: "Pulpit poofs can stay"', wrote the *Sun*.

In this climate Bennett spent the earlier part of the weekend on a visit to Cambridge denying to friends that he had written the preface; then he returned to the house where he lived alone, found his cat Tiddles had died in his absence, went back to his car in the garage, and gassed himself.

After his death no close friends emerged to mourn him, but a host of allies. As soon as they had got over their shock, they proclaimed him a martyr at the hand of ruthless liberals.

The difficulty for the traditionalist party was that their central cause, resistance to the ordination of women, was unpopular within the Church and almost incomprehensible outside it. The only way to make it palatable was to accuse their opponents of every other form of wrongdoing as well. To be fair, there was spontaneity as well as calculation in this move: morality and theology are conjoined in the religious imagination, so that, once you have convinced yourself that someone is theologically mistaken, their immorality follows naturally.

The chief victim of this new mode of argument was the Archbishop of York, John Habgood, who had denounced the preface before the author's suicide as the work of a bitter and disappointed man. What made this remark unforgivable was its palpable truth. Since it was made while Bennett was still alive and anonymous but remembered after he was exposed and dead, it seemed vicious and petty as well as true. It probably finished Habgood's chances of becoming Archbishop of Canterbury.

Derek Pattinson, who had commissioned the preface, and refused to cut it, survived unscathed. He defended himself by the convention that the anonymity of the preface-writer must be absolute. This convention, so far as one can tell, he invented himself. He had been Secretary General of the General Synod for nearly twenty years, since just after it had started, and called it sometimes, with proprietary pride, 'My Synod'. He dressed like Neville Chamberlain, but once took a woman journalist to a leather bar for an interview.

All of these things were possible in the culture of subterranean tolerance, where anything was allowed so long as it did not frighten the horses. Don't ask, don't tell, and never put anything in writing were the watchwords. But such an arrangement depended on unwritten codes, and after the Higton debacle those codes were smashed to bits. Lives lived within them were smashed up too.

The Standing Committee of the General Synod passed a motion entirely exonerating Pattinson at its first meeting after Bennett's suicide. Another motion was proposed expressing support for Runcie. The leader of the Anglo-Catholic faction, Brian Brindley, whom Runcie had thought a friend, argued successfully against it on the grounds that to pass such a motion would be a tacit admission that there had been criticism of Runcie. Everyone around the table knew perfectly well that Brindley was a fountain of malicious gossip who could not have let a day pass without stabbing an archbishop in the back.

About a year later, Brindley, a lonely man, was introduced to a young journalist in Reading, where he lived. He took the youth to supper at the Athenaeum, and later made a series of clumsy, sentimental passes at him. The journalist had come forearmed, with a concealed microphone, and after his own paper turned the story down he passed the tapes to the *News of the World*, which gave Brindley the full treatment: 'We name the Kinky Canon: Runcie's pervert pal exposed'. He refused to resign, on the humiliating grounds that all he had said was merely fantasy. Brindley had spent twenty years turning his church into a Gothic treasure trove with a congregation gathered from miles around. When his bishop, Richard Harries, had once visited, he was supplied with a peacock throne and vestments from Gammarelli's in Rome. Harries now stood by Brindley, appalled by the treachery he had suffered.

So the two evangelical members of the Synod's Standing Committee, David Holloway and Mrs Jill Dann, a former Lady Mayor of Cheltenham, sent all 400 members of the Synod photocopies of the *News of the World* article. Harries then learned that the press had other stories, and Brindley finally resigned.

He retired to Brighton and became a Roman Catholic layman: the Roman Catholic Church would never ordain a man of such flamboyant sexuality. Brindley died in 2001, part way through a seven-course dinner hosted at the Athenaeum by twelve of his friends, all male, and – Andrew was told by one of them – almost all gay. After the waiters removed the body the feast resumed. It emerged from his obituary that he had added 'Dominic' and 'Titus' to his given names.

David Holloway, Brindley's nemesis in church politics, but his brother in self-confidence and lack of scruple, lost his place in Synod altogether at the 1990 elections, which were otherwise a triumph for the Calvinist evangelicals: forty of them reached the House of Laity where they formed a coherent block that operated with disciplined efficiency. But Holloway was thrown out by the votes of his fellow clergy.

He learnt from the experience that God did not want the Church of England governed by the Synod at all, as he had supposed when he was a power there. Instead, he founded a Calvinist group called Reform, which was to become the dominant expression of conservative evangelicalism in England. Reform made much play with money in their propaganda. It introduced the idea that member parishes should withhold their diocesan quotas: the annual sum for which they are assessed by the diocese and which provides a growing proportion of the Church's income. The quota is an extraordinarily unpopular, and hence inefficient way to raise money, since even when parishes are paying far less than they cost central funds, it feels as if they are paying huge sums for nothing. The role of money in the crisis is something for a later chapter, but it first emerged as a political factor in the context of the homophobic revolt.

Derek Pattinson made it safely into retirement. He was knighted, and accepted for ordination by Graham Leonard without any formal examination, but his later years were dreadful. After his mother died his drinking became more flamboyant, and he moved a General Synod member named Barnaby Miln into his flat in Pimlico. Miln, who had been the youngest JP in England, had startled the Synod during the Higton debate when he announced that he was gay himself, despite having a wife and two children.

Pattinson, even in retirement, had a chauffeur – until the young man was killed buying cocaine for Miln; one of his closest friends, Patrick Gilbert, who ran the missionary society and publishing house SPCK, was disgraced for stealing very large sums on expenses and escaped with a suspended sentence for spending some of it on a fourteen-year-old boy. Miln established himself as a gay entrepreneur (he owned an escort agency) in Edinburgh and then moved back in with Pattinson in Pimlico. In due course, Pattinson left for a nursing home, where he died in 2006, and Miln set up in business in their old flat as a male prostitute specializing in sado-masochistic fantasies.

Miln once took Andrew to Pattinson's flat and showed him their bedroom, where the most prominent decoration was a curious silvery sculpture, framed and hanging on the wall. It turned out to be a plate from which had been printed the page of *The Times* announcing Derek's knighthood.

The Higton affair and the events around it greatly hastened the Church's uncoupling from English society. No one came out of it well. Loss of Parliamentary control proved not a liberation but a disaster, as church affairs moved from the broad stage of national affairs to the small one of church politics. The evangelicals' hatred of liberals and obsession with moral purity led them to bind the Church into a commitment to the values of the 1950s, despite these becoming increasingly unpalatable to the rest of society on moral grounds as well as more pragmatic ones. Anglo-Catholics let their opposition to women's ordination cloud their judgement, and exposed a nasty vein of clerical in-fighting over petty privileges and preferment. The 'don't ask, don't tell' policy by which church leaders had conducted church business for so long was exposed as hiding corruption of the sort evangelicals had long suspected. And the liberal elite failed to stand up to any of it. They had been so used to running the show that they underestimated the power of evangelicals operating in the context of the Synod and overestimated the elegant patrician power which they had exercised for so long. By the time they noticed how much just about everything had changed it was too late.

# 4

# A brief theory of religious decline

Up to this point we have introduced the old Church and the forces, internal and external, which were to change it for ever. Before we proceed to tell the cautionary tale of what happened next, it's worth making explicit the theory that underpins it all.

Religions are like rivers: very little of what matters is visible on the surface. They can scour deep gorges and flood vast tracts, but what determines their course are the deeper currents, and the ground over which they flow. If a river that has been deep and placid, with strange sluggish depths where monstrous catfish swim, plunges almost without warning into a cataract of froth and thunder and confusion, this is because the ground it flows across has changed from silt to rock. It isn't the waves on the surface that cause the motion underneath.

What brought the Church of England plunging downwards was a deep change in the society of which it had been part. To explain this it's necessary to step back into the understanding of religion as a social scientist or a historian might look at it. There are of course other ways to explain what has happened, such as the Calvinist understanding of a society, repeatedly punished because it has turned from God, which can only be saved by collective repentance. But that stopped being a belief that was acted on in the mid-nineteenth century. The last national day of fasting to recover God's favour was proclaimed in 1857, during the Indian Mutiny, and followed two in the preceding years which were directed at victory in the Crimean War.

One of the biggest social changes was the decline of paternalism, broadly understood to include not just the rule of men over women and children, but the idea that there are legitimate authorities which override the judgement and conscience of individuals, and to which they must defer. The opposite of paternalism is liberalism of the kind outlined by J. S. Mill, which holds that each and every individual is the best judge of what directly affects his or her own personal life, that this holds true even if they are in error, and that it should be limited only by the principle that the exercise of freedom should not harm others. By the first part of the new millennium 90 per cent of the British population subscribed to a liberal set of values: this was evident in their attitudes to issues like women's liberation, abortion, same-sex marriage and assisted dying. In most people's minds these fell into the category of it not being appropriate to tell other people how to lead their lives.

This was not a matter of abstract belief, but of everyday practice. To put that in the terms in which the pioneering oral historian Elizabeth Roberts once explained it, in the past when a lad was naughty at school, he was punished by the teacher, got a slap round the ear on the way home from the policeman who'd heard about it, and was then slippered by his dad. Social order was upheld by an interlocking set of authorities which supported one another. Sometime in the 1970s, they collapsed like a pack of cards.

Religious people often think that churches decline because people stop believing in God, but in fact belief ceases to seem credible when people no longer act on it. Rituals and routine practices construct their own meanings. It is the unspoken and inarticulable parts of religion which give it strength. The more 'religious' belief comes to be something distinct and separate from the normal beliefs and practices of the society around it, the more vulnerable it becomes. T. S. Eliot expressed this perfectly when he wrote that 'Bishops are a part of English culture, and horses and dogs are a part of English religion.'

The Church of England was for most of the twentieth century an extreme example of a societal church, one which sanctified and drew strength from the everyday lives of the people. The vicar was a part of society like the squire, the doctor or the milkman. You didn't have to be a member of the church to acknowledge this, any more than you have to be ill to know what a doctor is for.

But this is only one way for churches to function, and societal churches are different from congregational ones. The latter – which sociologists call 'sectarian' in a non-pejorative sense – draw a sharp divide between themselves and the rest of society, and distinguish members from non-members in terms of commitment, finances, piety, theology and salvation. Tony Higton's parish in Essex, though notionally Anglican, was actually run on entirely puritan-sectarian lines, with a really clear division between those who were in (and who donated 10 per cent of their income) and those who were out, unsaved, and deserving of God's dreadful wrath. The intensity of the war between some evangelicals and the rest of the clergy derived from the clash between their congregational model of church as a community of the saved separating itself from corruption, and the Anglican model of the church as largely unconcerned with corruption, and open to everyone.

Despite their natural dislike of one another, both kinds of churches draw their strength and nourishment from everything that happens outside church. They do so in very different and ultimately incompatible ways. Societal churches are sustained by the sense that they reinforce society; congregational ones by feeling in conflict with it. Anna Strhan's work on a conservative evangelical congregation in London shows this dynamic very clearly. The members feel themselves cut off and set apart socially as well as theologically; as Calvinists, they hope to be part of the small faithful remnant who are saved, while the rest of us are condemned to eternal torment. But at the same time they are conscious, sometimes painfully, that this belief makes them look crazy and rather unpleasant to the people around them. This increases their general sense of anxiety and doubt, which in turn reinforces their need for forgiveness, and for an atoning figure. The very beliefs which would seem to cut them off from society depend for their persistence on daily interaction with people who don't share them. (That's one reason for the divide between Calvinists and charismatics – as we will see, the charismatics are much more fluid about their beliefs, since what really matters is the ineffable content of the experience, so they feel much less cut off from the society around them.)

This linkage with wider society, and with ordinary, unreflective life, is the most important of three things that any social grouping or relationship, religious or not, requires to keep going. The other two are ritual and belief. In religious rituals, the essential nature of a religion is enacted in ways that cannot be contained in words. Nor can they be properly understood from the outside. It is the essence of a ritual that it changes the participants, who must perform their parts for this to work. Some of this is body language: kneeling in prayer, or standing to pray and sing, or putting your hands in the air. In Christianity, a great deal lies in the central rites of baptism in water, and eating bread and drinking wine. Some is the repetition of formulaic prayers and creeds, or singing together. Some is a matter of processions and attendance – Remembrance Day services, or midweek house groups and coffee mornings. But all of it is vitally important to the way religions and other communal structures of meaning are maintained. This is why gigantic quarrels will convulse churches when the pews are removed: changing the physical expression of worship alters what is being expressed; it changes what Christianity is in the lives of the worshippers.

The last and in some ways the least important of these three constituents of a religion is theology. Theology, in this sense, is how you explain what you are doing, both to yourself and to others. So it is dependent on what you actually do. This is a tremendously obvious insight which some forms of Christianity – and all forms of journalism – try more or less consciously to ignore. Pierre Bourdieu called it the 'scholastic fallacy' – the mistake which those who live in their heads make of assuming that everyone else does the same. In the context of upheavals of the social order, this dependence of theology on practice is especially important.

Talking about the relationship between practice, ritual and theology feels oddly like the fifth-century disputes about the nature of the Trinity. You need a language which makes clear that they all depend on each other, and all affect each other while having independent existences. What matters most is to remember that practice is not just the outworking of theory, but has its own logic.

This kind of 'three-legged stool' of practice, ritual and belief actually applies to all kinds of social relations, even to those between couples. Here their daily interactions are the practice, the rituals are sexual, and the theology, or the theory, is the stories they tell themselves and each other about the relationship. It's more obvious in this case that all three depend on each other. No one ever loved by an effort of thought and will alone, and the meaning of sex in a relationship is rooted in everything that happens outside the bed.

Religions are collective relationships. If you want to understand what is happening inside them, you have to observe behaviour and ritual quite as much as the stories that people tell you about them. So the deep changes in English behaviour brought about by women's changing place in society, by other outworkings of liberalism, and by the fall first of the empire and then of post-war utopianism were not societal intrusions into a theological world, as is implied by talk of a secular modern world clashing with religious 'tradition'; they were convulsions in the river bed of religion itself.

The success of the Church for so many centuries had lain in its ability to remain articulated with English society, not just by running alongside it like a page beside a stagecoach, but by helping it to sustain and comprehend itself. Religion, Durkheim said, is the place where a society holds before itself its better image – though perhaps he was being a bit optimistic. Nevertheless, at its strongest, the Church of England had been able to celebrate and comfort the English people (or at least those who didn't prefer to be 'non-conformist') in their deepest joys and sorrows, both individually and collectively. It was embedded in England's changing social structure, including its patternings and inequalities of class, race and gender – both maintained by and helping to maintain them.

You can see some of this when looking at what newspapers meant when they used to talk about 'traditionalists': the ideal of the changeless church with old ladies bicycling to communion through the morning mists, and bishops in their cathedrals, as they had been since the seventh century, was a profoundly social vision of who the English were. Jesus, after all, had nothing to say about bicycles. Bishops were part of English culture. But they had also been part of the English ruling class, had been to school with it, or university, or fought with it as officers in the war. The fact that a bishop in a later chapter shoots ducks off his moat tells you much more about the role of a bishop in the society in which he grew up than any amount of theology could. So when that class structure fell, as it seemed to under Mrs Thatcher, it brought the bishops down with it.

When a social order based around hierarchies of class, gender and age, and the central figure of the male provider, started to collapse, the stitches which threaded the everyday life of women and children into the local church and community started to come undone as well. A lot of churchgoing was down to habit, duty and social obligation. Far from being weak foundations for religion, they are the strongest of all. Life is part of religion, and religion is part of life. When the shape of life starts to dissolve and re-form, as it endlessly does, religion needs to flow along with it, not necessarily in slavish conformity, but in some sort of reasonable harmony. Only if everything changes can everything appear unchanging, the same from age to age.

This is what the Church of England failed to do. Faced with the challenge of maintaining a living relation between its traditions and the society of which it was part, it baulked. It had proved adept at transforming itself into a central part of the post-war welfare society, but the post-Thatcher settlement threw it completely. Rather than engage with what was happening, it started to mutter threats against the society of which it had been part, and to turn inwards. Clericalism increased, and internecine warfare between clerical tribes proved a destructive distraction. Rather than attempting to hold things together, leaders succumbed to the temptation of thinking that their brand of churchmanship held the solution, if only it could be imposed on the others. The theme of the remaining chapters is voodoo. Like a cargo cult, the leaders of 'the Church that was' resorted to ritual incantations, trumpet blasts and the manipulation of the outward form of things, rather than facing honestly what needed to be done.

# 5

# The trouble with women

The story so far has largely been about men, among them men who were worried about women, and men who were worried about men who were not real men. But away from the battlements and colleges and centres of power, it was women who still kept the Church going, as they had always done.

This made the battle over women's ordination both odd and peculiarly self-destructive. It wasn't just that women outnumbered men in the pews, and were more active and committed. It wasn't just that the Queen was Supreme Governor of the Church, deeply committed to it. It wasn't just that women arranged the flowers, dusted the pews and supported the parson. It was that through their work as teachers, nurses and volunteer workers, women wove the Church into the fabric of English life and, as mothers, passed its practices to the next generation.

Beyond the scenes sketched so far there was another Church of England which carried on largely oblivious of the Synod, Higton, scandals, and the increasingly bitter battle between conservatives and liberals. This was the local church, which baptized, married, conducted funerals, organized fetes and pageants, ran schools, rang bells and looked after roofs. It was the Church of England school, and the parish magazine. It was sung evensong on the radio, and the intangible church body to which people belonged, even if they never went, and to which they were ascribed by default: 'What religion are you? Don't know? I'll put CofE then.' It was a broad church which tended not to get too worked up about the divisions of churchmanship which mattered so much to clergy, especially clergy in London and large cities.

One effect of the battles which were fought first over women priests and then over the treatment of gay people was to introduce a new division into the Church: 'traditionalists' or 'conservatives' versus 'liberals'. Although it related to the old distinctions of high, low and broad churchmanship, which had to do with how you ran your church – the ritual, theology and ecclesiology – it was significantly different. The new division was very twentieth century. It was part of a 'culture war' which raged most intensely over issues of sex and gender, but which pitted a whole set of 'traditional' values against the alleged relativism of modern secular life. Its origins lay in the battles first waged by Christian fundamentalists in the USA against those they called 'liberals', a catch-all term for the agents and dupes of the 'secular modernity' they opposed.

Conservatives in Britain, both evangelical and Catholic, disliked the word 'fundamentalist' because it conjured up ideas of American crazies, so they used 'traditionalist' or 'conservative' instead, and presented themselves as the defenders of 'orthodoxy' and 'Biblical

Truth'. In fact the 'traditionalist' label was misleading, given how changing and varied Anglican tradition had been; given also that it had included powerful women leaders from Elizabeth I to Elizabeth II, so those who used it to oppose women's leadership had to shut one eye to block out most of Anglican history as well as what really went on in many parishes.

Unlike American denominations, which are associations of independent congregations, the Church of England had always been both congregational and national; it couldn't have succeeded as the latter if it hadn't also been the former. Its parochial system parcels out the whole of the country in small units which have traditionally been served by one or more resident clergymen responsible for the souls of all who live within the parish. Historically, the parish was the basic financial as well as territorial unit of the Church. Endowments were never given to the Church as a body, nor to dioceses: they were given to endow a bishopric, a parish, a monastery, a capitular body, a school, almshouse or some other charitable institution. Until the twentieth century, expenses of the parishes were met from church rights and by patrons. Each parish priest managed his own affairs. The natural result was what the report of the Archbishops' Committee on Church Finance of 1911 considered 'an exaggerated parochialism'. Rural parish churches exist alongside the greater churches and cathedrals of the towns and cities. Everyone belongs to a parish, like it or not – and quite understandably a lot of non-conformists and Catholics don't.

Although there was a lot of agonizing among Victorian clergymen about the difficulty of adapting this system to an increasingly urban society, the Church of England coped rather well by providing many of the services required by an industrial order: mass education, healthcare, philanthropy. This was largely thanks to its women, for behind these 'works of benevolence' was an army of largely middle-class Anglican laywomen and members of religious orders, supported by wealthy lay donors and patrons. They helped run hospitals, nurse and teacher training, primary and secondary schools, temperance and 'uplift' movements, local visiting schemes, education and support for mothers and babies, homes for unmarried mothers, and pioneering schemes for what we would now call public health and social medicine – as well as missions abroad.

Today we only remember a few of the most prominent names in this remarkable episode of church history – Florence Nightingale, Josephine Butler, Catherine Booth, Charlotte Mason, Edith Cavell. Most are forgotten and uncelebrated. The amnesia helped pave the way for the 'traditionalist' denial of women's leadership.

Its immediate cause was the way in which both Church and state had turned their backs on women's volunteer work in their early enthusiasm for a welfare state run on more scientific lines, preferably by men. In 1946 the bishops closed down the system of local parish visitors, whereby organized teams of women visited the sick and lonely. After the war a more professional and highly paid clergy took over a small element of the more interesting work done by women, and professionals in the welfare state did the rest. Missions overseas were closing, and 'charity' and 'benevolence' went out of favour.

Opportunities for Anglican laywomen to contribute through work for the Church shrank accordingly. Women who would once have considered teaching or nursing or some other form of caring work as their Christian calling started to think of themselves as secular professionals instead. Social policy took the place of theology. Religious Instruction in schools gave way to more multicultural forms of Religious Education. Anglican teacher-training institutions closed. In the process the Church lost many of its most important insertion points into everyday English life.

Barbara Pym's novels set in the 1950s capture the tail-end of this era, preserving a world of middle-class Anglican women already in decline. The life of many of her characters, like Wilmet Forsyth in *A Glass of Blessings*, revolves around parish and clergy, home and family; the former provide the social interest which sustains the latter. Wilmet still visits a church 'Settlement' in a poorer part of London, but council houses are being built around it, and the agnostic Sybil has taken over the committee meetings.

Sybil shudders at old Lady Nollard's talk of 'the lower classes' and 'the poor', and frowns on her recollections of 'the nourishing soup or broth we used to make for the cottagers on the estate'. Wilmet is aware that even the parish clergy are a little past their glory. She sighs at the decline in the quality of sermons, noting how they are no longer adorned with great literary quotations, but reduced to 'ten minutes' rather dry teaching on such topics as "The Significance of Evensong", or little nagging perorations about why we ought to go to confession'. But the parish remains the centre of her social life, with women and clergy revolving around one another, and both revolving around the feasts and fasts of the old liturgical year.

This kind of symbiosis between clergy and laywomen existed at the opposite end of the social spectrum as well. Ellen Clark-King, one of the first women priests, moved to a parish in the old shipbuilding part of Newcastle upon Tyne in 2000. Like many nineteenth-century churches, the church there had been built by someone from the higher classes to improve the morals of the lower ones. It had a parish school called 'Feed my Sheep'. Clark-King recorded the voices of the last generation of women to sustain it, already elderly at the time.

In this matrifocal society, church still offered the comforting, supportive presence of a Father God who helped the women get through the tragedies and hardships of tough lives, and made up for the deficiencies of their real men: 'I mean, me divorce and all different things like that and He's just pulled me through it … 'cos I never, I never had the strength to do it myself.' These women believe in heaven and hell, look forward to meeting their loved ones again, and are aware of the presence of the dead around them: 'When my mother died, this house went icy cold … It was dead, cold and dead, for a whole month. And then something happened … no sunshine outside, but the whole place was lit up. And we always said that she was back again and would never leave it.'

These women don't begrudge their daughters the opportunities they never had, but they know that these spell the end of the Church: 'In the old days [women] used to keep the church running, the men were the figureheads. We haven't even got figureheads now as men, and we haven't got the women quietly beavering away in the background.'

In the countryside, women also kept the Church alive, in much more broad church settings. In Linda's Anglican-by-default upbringing in west Somerset in the 1970s, men played virtually no part. Her faith derived in part from family – in the attenuated form of prayers at bedtime and the knowledge that she'd been baptized – and in part from Church of England primary school. This two-room Victorian building opposite the village church was run by Mrs Everett the head teacher, Mrs Williams the junior teacher, and Mrs Meals (truly) the dinner lady. Every morning Mrs Everett read a Bible story and Mrs Williams played a hymn. They had a limited repertoire, but the comfortable repetition worked the stories and hymns into the marrow of childish bones. They selected stories like the boy Samuel called by God, and Zacchaeus the tax collector called down from his tree by Jesus. These made children feel special – as if God might call them too, despite the fact that they were still in Clarks sandals. You just had to be alert. The lesson from the Good Samaritan was that we should be kind to everyone within reason (even Jehovah's Witnesses), and the lesson from Jesus that some things were worth dying for. It all struck Linda as true at age six, and still does today.

The church across the road played a more limited role. Nearly everyone in the parish trooped there for Harvest Festival, Christmas and Easter. These were still largely pagan festivals, which involved dragging large amounts of vegetable matter into church – gourds and corn dollies for Harvest, holly and fir for Christmas, and sacks of damp moss for the Easter garden. The gathering from hedgerows and woods was fun, and the look and smell in church with candles lit was magical. It enhanced that sense of the mystery of things which came easily with childhoods spent on farms, in contact with the spirits which dwelt in glassy ponds and hollow trees, stirring just below the surface.

The likes of John Stott or Brian Brindley were utterly alien to this world of what Winston Churchill called 'county council religion'. If this way of life was starting to erode by the 1980s, it was partly because of the breaking up of the local by wider forces like increased education and mobility, and partly because of the ways in which women's lives were changing. The increasingly heated disputes over the ordination of women were even having an impact: not only were they reported in the papers, but the politicking around them started to seep down to the parishes.

A few prominent laywomen were opposed to the ordination of women, and were celebrated by male traditionalists as proof that it wasn't all a male plot. Margaret Hewitt, who led 'Women against the Ordination of Women' and became famous for her hats, spoke on their behalf. From a different end of the class spectrum, one of Ellen Clark-King's Newcastle parishioners explained her own objections like this: 'A lot of people seem to think that it would be nice to have women priests but I'm, I'm from the old school and I – with all due respect Ellen, honestly – I just think that, you know, a man, usually, is the priest. I'm talking about our faith, our church, Ellen, with all due respect to you, honestly please.'

Overall, however, opponents of women's ordination, both male and female, were in a minority among laypeople. By the late 1970s over 80 per cent of Anglicans were expressing support for the statement: 'Women should be able to become members of the clergy.' The proportion was a bit lower among regular churchgoers, but there was still a healthy majority in favour.

Over time, a majority of bishops had also come to favour the change. They were strengthened by Donald Coggan, Archbishop of

Canterbury between 1974 and 1980, a powerful spokesman for the cause. 'How long can you cripple the church by letting your women … serve as parish workers, but not entrust them on a big scale?' he asked his fellow clergy.

So it was a minority who blocked women's ordination when it came to a vote, but they blocked it hard. Once General Synod came into being in 1970, that became the major forum for dealing – or not dealing – with the issue, and it became clear that it was the House of Clergy within the Synod which was the obstacle to change. Time and again, the necessary two-thirds majority proved elusive.

It had taken the Church of England a long time even to get to this point. The Salvation Army had commissioned women as officers since the late nineteenth century, and most other Protestant denominations in England had gradually followed their example. So had the Lutheran state churches in Scandinavia which the Church of England most closely resembled. The Methodists' decision to ordain women was a major reason why well-developed proposals for union were eventually rejected by the Church of England. But the Roman Catholic and Orthodox Churches remained resolutely opposed, and the Catholic wing of Anglican clergy still cared more about them than about all the others put together.

The moves of other churches within the Anglican Communion itself were, however, harder to ignore, and not for the first time it was they who kindled change back in England.

In 1944, against the background of war, Florence Li Tim-Oi had become the first woman to be ordained priest in the Anglican Church, in the diocese of Hong Kong and South China. She had converted to Christianity as a student, naming herself in honour of Florence Nightingale. In 1941, after four years of theological training, she was ordained deacon – something not then possible in England – and given charge of the Anglican congregation in the Portuguese colony of Macao. When the Sino-Japanese war led to a flow of refugees into this congregation while simultaneously making it too dangerous for priests to travel there to assist, the bishop of Hong Kong, Ronald Hall, ordained 'Florence Lee' priest in order to allow her to administer the sacraments.

This was not the careless act of a desperate bishop. Florence was talented and well trained, and she stood in the long tradition of Anglican women's ministry and mission. Both she and Hall were influenced by the established practice in China of indigenizing the Church, which gave them a critical perspective on English Anglican culture. They considered themselves less socially conservative. Hall, raised in a vicarage in a working-class part of Newcastle, trained at Brasenose and Cuddesdon, and, decorated with a Military Cross in the First World War, was a political radical who had supported the Chinese revolution, and who would later play an important role in the reconstruction of Hong Kong. What happened in 1944 was part of a considered direction of travel, not a mere accident.

This was not how it was received in England. The *Church Times* called Hall a 'wild man of the woods' who had gone native and strayed beyond the limits of civilized behaviour by failing to subject himself to constitutional authority and due process. Archbishop William Temple, to whom Hall had written personally, stalled before replying, admitting that 'if we could find any shadow of theological ground for the non-ordination of women I should be immensely comforted, but such arguments as I have heard on that line seem quite desperately futile'. His written objection to Hall, when it came, was that the bishop had proceeded *ultra vires*, contrary to all the laws and precedents of the Church, and that his action was deplorable.

Li Tim-Oi was forced to 'resign'. The Lambeth Conference of 1948 responded by reasserting its long-standing opposition to women entering Holy Orders. Hall counselled angry campaigners for women's ordination against raising the issue again at the Lambeth Conference of 1958. He considered it a waste of time, and thought that unilateral action by a national church was the best way forward. In his view the Chinese bishops should have stood firm and said: 'We propose to let the Rev. Florence Lee exercise her Ministry and will report again at the next [Lambeth] Conference on the progress of the experiment. We ask you not to excommunicate us for taking this step.'

Against this backdrop and the liberalizing movements of the 1960s, including the Second Vatican Council, the Church of England continued to work busily for no change by commissioning a series of reports which reached indecisive conclusions. One, issued in 1962, reported that it was 'unable to express any opinion whether the Church as a whole wants or does not want women in priests' orders'.

Hall was right that English opposition would only be shaken by a blast from outside its walls, but the way in which it occurred was unexpected. As he had hoped, Hong Kong became the first diocese to ordain women, but it did so in a perfectly legal fashion: to everyone's astonishment the Anglican Consultative Council of 1971 gave the green light.

The 'ACC' had been brought into being by the 1968 Lambeth Conference as a more efficient way of dealing with issues facing the whole Communion. It was constituted along uncharacteristically democratic lines for an Anglican body, with member churches represented not just by a bishop, but by an elected priest, layman, and woman observer – who could speak. At the Council's first meeting in Limuru, Kenya, in 1971, it had to consider a request from Hall's successor as bishop of Hong Kong for advice on how he should proceed with regard to women's ordination. By a slim margin, the Council passed a motion which said that if the bishop of Hong Kong decided to ordain women 'his action will be acceptable to the Council'. So he did. Immediately.

There was a chain reaction. The English bishops were horrified. The status of the ACC was rapidly downgraded to prevent further mishaps. Supporters of women's ordination in the Episcopal Church of the USA were delighted. They tabled a motion at their National Convention in 1973 asking for canons to be passed allowing them to do the same, and were furious when the motion was defeated. This anger propelled four bishops, three of them retired, to break ranks and ordain eleven women illegally in 1974 – the so-called 'Philadelphia Eleven'. The following year the Canadian Anglican General Synod officially approved the ordination of women. The American church followed suit the year after. Some women deacons moved from Britain to the USA to be ordained there. Jack Spong, bishop of Newark, and Graham Leonard, bishop of London, became locked in a symbolic battle between ancient colonial oppression and wanton modern liberalism – or so it seemed to them.

Back in England, the fact that colonies had taken a stand against the mother church did nothing to change opponents' minds. But they were faced with the embarrassing question of how ordained women visiting Britain should be treated. It was customary for an Anglican priest in good standing with his local bishop to have his orders recognized, and to be allowed to celebrate the Eucharist throughout the Anglican Communion. So the bishops faced a dilemma: annoy brother bishops, or annoy the Roman Catholic and Orthodox Churches. They decided that the former would be preferable, and Synod agreed. They weren't bothered about annoying Methodists and other Free Churches in Britain, nor their close cousins the Scandinavian churches, who had by now been ordaining women for years.

In 1985, however, the Church of England took a step which inadvertently hastened the ordination of women. It agreed to ordain women as deacons. This meant that women became clergy for the first time ('deaconesses' in England being lay). Opponents hoped that this would dampen demands for ordination to the priesthood, but it had the opposite effect. Because women could now do just about everything a priest could, except bless, absolve from sin, and celebrate the Eucharist, it made the abnormal spectacle of women doing sacred things start to seem normal.

By this point, positions had become entrenched, and propaganda and counter-propaganda were flying all over the place. Linda remembers a friend's husband being converted to the cause of women's ordination by a leaflet posted through the door which listed twenty-seven objections to women priests. 'Had there been one or two I would have remained opposed,' he said. But twenty-seven looked desperate.

The argument about not derailing hopes of Anglican–Catholic unity was still being used, but had become a damp squib ever since the conservative John Paul II had made it clear that, while he was happy to share photo opportunities with Archbishops of Canterbury, he had little interest in getting any closer. 'It was like a submarine coming up through a trawler and the whole thing sinks. And the awful thing is how no one seems to care,' George Austin, the archdeacon of York and a substantial opponent in Synod, later recalled. Theological arguments had for a long time been deflated by the fact that the Church had admitted there were no serious objections to women's ordination. And arguments about the essentially different nature of men and women didn't play particularly well in the context of a society which had now made sex discrimination illegal.

Opponents fell back on trying to frighten people. They suggested that the ordination of women would be a capitulation to the forces of liberalism, a Pandora's box out of which would pop all sorts of horrors, including women bishops, practising homosexuals (possibly even lesbians), pagan liturgies, goddess worship, moral decay and church decline. They also claimed that if the measure passed, the Church of England would split in two: a traditionalist church, and a liberal one. Thousands upon thousands of Anglicans would defect and leave for Rome.

These suggestions seem to have genuinely terrified the Anglican bishops – and, briefly, to have made Cardinal Basil Hume so excited that he started talking unguardedly about 'the conversion of England'.

That anyone seriously believed any of this now seems mystifying. It reveals the gulf which had opened between church leaders, laypeople and parishes, and it implicates the press, which operated like a hall of distorting mirrors.

There was a tragic side as well. Some of the 'traditionalists' were genuinely heartbroken that the Church they had loved and served was about to be changed for ever. But the price paid by their opponents was always higher, because while it's bad to have your home ransacked, it's much worse to stand outside in the cold pleading for admission, while being alternately ignored and pelted with stones.

Some of the women who had campaigned their whole lives literally died waiting – like Phoebe Willett, who celebrated the Eucharist jointly, and illegally, with her clergy husband shortly before her death from cancer. When an early motion was defeated in the Synod in 1978, Una Kroll had famously cried out from the public gallery: 'We asked for bread and you gave us a stone.'

The situation was particularly difficult for the growing number of women who wanted to be ordained. By the early 1990s there was a queue of 1,200 women deacons waiting to become priests. Not only did many have to put up with appalling treatment from a poisonous minority of genuine misogynists, but they couldn't afford to retaliate because their opponents would declare them unchristian, unwomanly and unfit for ordination.

Not surprisingly, therefore, the tone of the campaign for women's ordination was extraordinarily mild. Kroll's scriptural outburst was about as outrageous as it got. Looking back now on the stack of books and essays produced at the time, what's striking is their cautious and reasoned approach, how carefully they turn over the scriptural, theological and ecclesiological evidence to make their case, how courteously they deal with objections. Far from being 'radical' or 'pagan', Anglican feminist theologians clung tenaciously to the tradition, and remained firmly within the bounds of orthodoxy – in contrast to the much wilder and more exciting theological excursions of Mary Daly and Starhawk in the US, and Daphne Hampson in the UK. In the end so much damage was done, and so much hurt inflicted in the final stages of the battle, that the victory for women, when it came at the Synod meeting of November 1992, was bittersweet for everyone.

George Carey, by then Archbishop, was clear and unwavering in his support for women's ministry. It was left to the suaver Habgood, Archbishop of York, to deal with the opponents. Addressing the Synod, Carey said: 'God calls us to take the risk of faith. I believe that God is also calling his Church to ordain women to the priesthood.' After some forty more speeches, the vote was taken. The result in both the House of Laity and of Clergy was so close that it took a while to work out the maths. But the requisite two-thirds majority in all three Houses had been reached – just. One laywoman (the wife of an Anglo-Catholic priest) who had been expected to vote 'no' had remained rooted to her seat in floods of tears. Another, the Dean of the Arches, who had been expected to abstain, was seen entering the 'yes' lobby. That this was pored over showed how close it had been.

Opponents immediately declared the victory weak and 'disappointing'. Supporters were warned not to rejoice – a theme that would be played out again and again in the coming years. And there were some major snags in the legislation which meant that the women didn't have quite as much to celebrate as they would have liked.

Unlike most other Anglican churches, the Church of England had not passed a motion allowing for women to be admitted to Holy Orders on the same terms as men. They could become priests, but not bishops. This disastrous half-measure meant that before long the battle over women would be cranked up all over again, and the Church would suffer another twenty years of wrangling. By that time the rest of the country would have lost interest.

The legislation had also left hanging the question of how opponents would be compensated. This, rather than the future of women and the Church, took up the bishops' immediate attention. Considerable care was taken to make sure that the cost of conscience for traditionalists should be as low as possible. Members of the Parliamentary Ecclesiastical Committee, which vets church legislation before it comes before Parliament, joined in the efforts.

The solution was arrived at in an uncharacteristically timely and helpful manner. Male priests who wanted to leave would be compensated with a generous financial package. In the event, only 250 left between 1994 and 2000, with numbers slowing to a trickle thereafter, despite the eventual foundation by Pope Benedict of a Catholic Ordinariate to receive them. As noted before, by 2014 the total number who had 'gone across' amounted to around four hundred, rather than the thousands predicted.

In addition, a system of 'alternative episcopal oversight' was put in place. This consisted of three 'flying bishops' to whom opponents of women's ordination could look if they objected to dealing with their own diocesan bishop on the grounds that he had been tainted by ordaining women; in the context of the Aids epidemic, the metaphor of contagion was a powerful one. The bishops also hoped to ensure that dioceses would have at least one untainted bishop available. In London, for example, David Hope, who had succeeded Graham Leonard as the diocesan bishop, decided to sit it out when women were ordained, and let one of his suffragan bishops do the deed. His successor, Richard Chartres, ordained all deacons, but no priests of either sex.

A few opponents fought on, particularly in London, which had always been the main centre of opposition. One of the most dogged, the Revd Paul Williamson, launched a series of legal cases against the Church. His most famous attempt to have both archbishops arraigned for treason was brought to an end by Justice Popplewell, who pronounced 'the argument – if I can dignify it by using the word – […] the most far-fetched I have ever heard'. Undaunted, Mr Williamson announced that he was planning to sue for one-third of the assets of the Church of England, on behalf of the Synod members who had lost the vote: 'Every third cathedral in England will be mine.' When the ordination services of women began, Williamson was given permission to lodge a protest against the illegality of one of the first in St Paul's Cathedral. Two decades later, at the consecration of the first woman bishop, Williamson was at it again, objecting on biblical grounds when the congregation was asked to assent to the consecration. His objection was formally dismissed.

The decision to ordain women as priests but not bishops was too little, too late. The convulsions which led up to it, and the rift they caused with the increasingly settled practice and conviction of a country which had by then elected a woman Prime Minister, did enormous harm.

Despite the sensitive measures taken to accommodate opponents of women's ordination, one of the casualties was the Anglo-Catholic party itself. The long tradition of Anglo-Catholic parishes sustained by women's devotion came to a shuddering halt. It was a shock for Anglo-Catholic women, at either end of the class spectrum, to realize that many of the clergymen they had supported seemed to hate them so much. Some of these women stayed out of loyalty, but their daughters left. In Britain the children of Anglicans became increasingly likely to abandon the faith of their parents and grandparents and snap the chain of tradition.

The dispute also consolidated the destructive division between traditionalists and liberals, which would continue to play out in relation to gay people. Older groups like the Church Union were eclipsed first by the Anglo-Catholic 'Cost of Conscience' movement, which became 'Forward in Faith', and then by 'Reform'. This signalled the shift in control of the traditionalist agenda from the waning Anglo-Catholics to the conservative evangelicals. It was all a long way from the more truly traditional sense that Anglo-Catholic, evangelical and liberal were different and mutually balancing emphases within core Prayer Book devotion and doctrine. One thing the infamous *Crockford's* preface got right was the weakening of the idea of Anglicanism once the Prayer Book had gone.

But the biggest casualty of the battle over women was the continuing support of ordinary English women, and their willingness to pass on the faith. The timing could not have been worse. The first generation of women to be both highly educated *and* still committed to the Church of England in large numbers was precisely the one the battle did most to alienate.

# 6

# Carey and managerial voodoo

The way George Carey handled the dispute over women's ordination revealed a lot about him. He considered the issue straightforward. He saw no theological objection to women priests, didn't understand the Anglo-Catholics, and couldn't see what the problem was. He liked strong women and was married to one. So he threw his weight behind the cause, allowed the trickier bishops to deal with the trickier people, and achieved what he considered to be the right result.

Like the blunt-talking, common-sense school of evangelicalism from which he came, Carey preferred things plain. He thought that a reasonable God had created an orderly world, and he looked for coherence. He saw in black and white rather than subtle shades of grey, and seemed a natural enemy of the verse by Emily Dickinson beloved of liberals: 'Tell the truth but tell it slant / Success in Circuit lies.' When Carey thought something was right or wrong, he liked to say so, and to act.

None of this made him popular in high-class Anglican circles. There was a lot of sneering. Carey was a world away from the cultivated sophistication of the bishops at Windsor. That was part of his appeal to Mrs Thatcher, who selected his name for appointment as Archbishop of Canterbury, though she was later said to be disappointed in how he turned out. Her initial support only deepened his detractors' gloom. Over sherry at Cuddesdon in 1991, a college governor ruminated on the vulgarity of his enthronement ceremony, and summed up the mood with a sigh: 'One feels rather dismayed.'

But Carey's confidence in his own ability to Know the Truth – as the title of his autobiography later put it – combined with a ponderous speaking style, and complete lack of irony, made him oddly out of place in the decade of Bill Clinton, Tony Blair and New Labour. Like the church he headed, he seemed a throwback to the 1970s or earlier, a time traveller who had unexpectedly landed in the middle of the 'Cool Britannia' party.

Carey was prone to what journalists call 'gaffes', in which a public figure says something obviously true in an unexpected setting. Almost the first thing he said in public after being appointed was that it was 'a serious heresy' to suppose that only a man could represent Christ at the altar. Given that this was the position of the Roman Catholic Church, the Orthodox Church, and around 10 per cent of his own Church, it was the first in a long list of things that an archbishop should not have said.

Carey's rise to the top had been rapid and unforeseen. He was the evangelical party's candidate, and his chief virtue in Mrs Thatcher's eyes was that he wasn't Runcie or Habgood. He had previously been bishop of Bath and Wells for less than two years (Runcie had consecrated him in the middle of the *Crockford's* crisis). His immediate predecessor, John Bickersteth, owed his advancement to his excellent shooting skills: as a young man he had impressed Prince Philip by bringing down three geese while on chaplaincy duty at Sandringham, and he later saw nothing odd in shooting the ducks off the moat that surrounded the bishop's palace. Carey was neither languid, nor socially self-assured. He had been born in Dagenham, where a cry of 'My bird!' did not mean the same as it did in Sandringham.

Although he came from a slightly higher social status than Runcie (his father was in more regular employment), he lacked Runcie's formation as a scholarship boy, an officer in an elite wartime regiment, and then an Oxbridge don. Carey, brought up on a council estate, educated at a secondary modern, and who did his national service in the peacetime RAF, never remotely acquired Runcie's ease with the old ruling class.

This added to his appeal for the evangelical party which supported him. He marked the decisive break with the old ethos of subtle evasions, studied ambiguities and the gentlemanly culture of 'don't ask, don't tell'. He absolutely did not do camp, and when he was pretentious he was entirely unconscious of it. He expected other people to share his reverence for the office of Archbishop of Canterbury and in this was constantly disappointed, except when he travelled abroad. In general, it can be said that he had the courage to be right and decisive about almost all the problems facing the Church, but the misfortune to be just as decisively wrong about most of the answers.

Christianity had given Carey's life shape and purpose, after he discovered it at the age of sixteen. The Church of England had lifted him from tedious and horrible jobs to well-respected and interesting ones. He had very little understanding for people who couldn't see how wonderful the gospel and its messengers were. This blindness to the thought processes of the people they are trying to convert is common among evangelicals, but in an archbishop it is something of a handicap.

He had been the vigorous and inspiring vicar of a large student church in Durham; a lecturer at Oak Hill, the conservative evangelical theological college; Principal of Trinity College, Bristol; a competent and energetic diocesan bishop. One-to-one and in small groups he was excellent: clear and forceful. Addressing large audiences, he deployed pompous and uplifting waffle and when this had no effect he said the same things more often and more loudly. He gave his first televised New Year's message in a woolly sweater rather than a cassock, which occasioned further mockery. Not much of this was his fault.

Even before he had taken office, Carey told the *Readers' Digest* that unless something was done, the Church would be in the position of 'A toothless old woman muttering in a corner, ignored by everyone.' It was a fine example of his ability to frame the problem vividly but not in a way that offered a plausible solution.

Carey's solution was to proclaim a 'Decade of Evangelism' to address the Church's decline. The idea derived from a resolution at the Lambeth Conference of 1988, and was provoked by reflection on the state of the Church as it approached the end of the second millennium Anno Domini. 'Mission' became the watchword in the Church of England, and a central 'Springboard' team was set up by the Archbishops of York and Canterbury to help dioceses and parishes get into gear.

By the time the initiative reached parish level, at least in the northern town where by the early 1990s Linda was a vicar's wife, the only impact was the arrival of a large envelope containing mission materials and cassette tapes of Carey chatting, and the visit of a single travelling preacher. A smart accountant from the south, he tried to convince a surprised congregation about the importance of mission by recounting a set of personal anecdotes about how his life had been changed by Jesus. He had a nice cup of tea with everyone at the end, and no more was said about it.

Carey took refuge from the scorn of the elites, and the sniggering of some of his bishops, in the things he understood. He wanted an end to corruption of all sorts, and thought the Church should be turned into a more effective organization. In case the preceding chapters haven't made this clear, the Church had never been an organization up till then, and seldom attained even the relative unity of a federation of organizations.

Organizations are means to ends, usually profit and product. They change all the time in order to deliver their results more efficiently. Churches, by contrast, are institutions – like families or Crufts – and institutions are more likely to be treated by those who belong to them as ends in themselves. Someone called them 'reluctant organizations'. They have the aura of something sacred, favour stability and permanence, and dislike interference and change. Their members feel a sense of ownership and belonging, and cherish their particular roles and niches within the institution. When that institution is a church, threats can be countered by erecting walls of dogma and digging in for God.

In the case of the Church of England, the complexity typical of an institution is multiplied by its antiquity, linkages with state and society, diocesan and parish system, connection to other churches in the Communion, and scale. Because of the pull towards permanence, new bodies and customs, once established, tend to persist, even when they have attained zombie status. Those who would like to close them can rarely muster the same level of endurance and steely determination as their defenders. As a consequence, absolutely everyone in the Church of England – from archbishop to person in the pew – feels powerless. Everyone suspects that some other bugger has more power than they do. It's a recipe for paranoia, paralysis and multiplying complexity.

Hinduism is easier to explain to students than the Church of England. Hardly anyone in the Church understands the whole of it, and if you try to produce an 'organogram' of the Church of England you quickly run out of patience and whiteboard.

You might start with the parishes. There are about 16,000 of them, with around 7,800 full-time paid ('stipendiary') clergy at the time of writing, one in five of whom are women, many now responsible for multiple parishes. Each parish has a Parochial Church Council – with around 150,000 people serving on 'PCCs' in total. Parishes are grouped into rural deaneries led by a rural or area dean. Above them are archdeaconries led by archdeacons, who are titled 'the Venerable'.

Parishes, deaneries and archdeaconries nest within a diocese, of which there were forty-four at the time Carey took office. Each diocese is headed by a bishop, who is assisted by area bishops, assistant bishops and suffragan bishops, who have lesser status than proper bishops but the same title ('the Right Reverend'). Each bishop has his own assistant staff, and diocesan staff typically occupy several floors of a substantial building. Dioceses are small empires in their own right, ruled by their bishops – who feel powerless. The two archbishops – of Canterbury and York – are officially just 'top bishops', *primus inter pares*. But they have even larger palaces, staffs and empires than diocesan bishops, and they are titled 'Most Reverend'.

Together, diocesan bishops and the two archbishops make up the House of Bishops, a section of the Synod but also a powerful body in its own right which talks, issues reports and sometimes makes decisions. Few suffragan, assistant and area bishops belong to the House of Bishops, unless elected there, but all belong to a larger and less powerful body called the College of Bishops, composed of all serving bishops.

Then there are the cathedrals. These are largely autonomous and separate from dioceses and their bishops, in terms of control, history and ethos. They have been unexpectedly successful in rejuvenating themselves in the last few decades. Despite recent reforms in their governance, they are still run by deans and canons, a system which derives from their (mostly) monastic origins. Each cathedral is fiercely independent. It is the mother church of the diocese and hosts bishops and parishes for certain events, but tends to keep them at arm's length. In the past, bishops didn't have full control over parishes or their clergy, because many were controlled by other 'patrons' – like the Queen, Oxbridge Colleges, local landholders, and Evangelical Patronage Trusts – and because parish clergy had 'freehold' which made them virtually untouchable. The parish priest was a little king in his own kingdom, hence the word interregnum to describe the interval when a parish has no clergyperson: 'between reigns'.

The next bit of the diagram is Parliament, which used to have ultimate control over the Church, along with the monarch and of course God. 'The only representatives of that Church of England are those who created the Church of England by establishing it by law, namely, this House,' said Enoch Powell in a Commons debate in the 1970s, battling a measure which gave the Church control over its own liturgy. But Parliament ignored Powell and gradually handed more power to the Church to run its own affairs. Parliament retains the power to approve measures taken in Synod ('Acts of Synod' have no legal status), so the Church can't wholly do as it pleases.

The Church's connection to Parliament also exists by way of the twenty-four senior bishops and two archbishops who are members of the House of Lords. At the top of the whole hierarchy is the monarch, the Supreme Governor of the Church of England, who may, like Elizabeth II, play a very active role in the Church, not just constitutionally, but as a sort of sacred goddess on the bowsprit.

Church House, the central bureaucracy of the CofE, is another major part of the institution. Housed in serious-looking, purpose-built buildings behind Westminster Abbey, it was opened by the Queen in 1940, and looks like the HQ of any other national institution of the time – a trades union perhaps, or the Post Office. It is staffed by clergy-with-promise and full-time church bureaucrats (many of them diligent and committed), and has its own debating chamber and departments, just like a mini-version of the real government in Westminster and Whitehall. Within it some act with an even greater sense of self-importance and detached aloofness than their secular counterparts, but to less purpose. Linda was once a member of the Higher Education Committee of the Board of Education. 'This is the most ineffectual committee you will ever serve on,' warned the chairman, a retired Vice Chancellor. And so it proved.

The Church Commissioners constitute another part of the organism. In Carey's time they were still housed in a grand Edwardian building at 1 Millbank, and considered themselves a cut above the Church House bureaucrats because they were part of the real civil service. They'd been reconstituted in 1948 out of the merging of the Ecclesiastical Commissioners and Queen Anne's Bounty: ancient church landholdings and investments were vested in them by Parliament in an attempt to centralize and rationalize the management of this public asset. They answered to Parliament, and had a deliberately arm's-length relationship with the rest of the Church.

The General Synod, already introduced, adds another level of complexity. Although it was meant to inject democracy into the Church, the bishops at the time of its creation didn't like the sound of that at all, because they didn't trust laypeople, and didn't want to give them too much power. The result, as we have seen, was the compromise in which the archbishops and bishops represent themselves and have a third of the votes, the clergy elect the clergy and have a third of the votes, and laypeople get elected by an arcane system based around deanery synods (which have little other purpose), and get the final third of the vote. For a really important motion to pass, it needs a two-thirds majority in all three Houses, meaning in effect that each House has a veto over the other two.

This arrangement has proved consistently effective in excluding from consideration the views of the majority of Anglicans.

Because the Synod is now the closest the Church gets to some sort of representative body, really big decisions – like whether to ordain women – end their journey there. This makes change difficult to achieve. The Synod now meets two or three times a year, at considerable expense, alternating between York and London; in the 1990s it always met three times annually.

If you try to connect all these parts of the Church to one another with arrows, you soon create a bewildering spider's web. It is much worse if you then try to add in all the additional parts of the Church, which have loose connections with some of the bits mentioned so far. There are things like Lambeth Palace and the Anglican Communion office, as well as various brainchildren and remnants of brainchildren of various archbishops and committees, such as the Church Urban Fund established as a result of *Faith in the City*. There are also many, many, many working groups and sub-committees. And beyond these central bodies there are 4,601 Church of England primary and secondary schools; chaplaincies in prisons, hospitals, universities, community centres and the armed forces; ecumenical projects; higher and further education institutions; trusts and charities; theological colleges and courses for training clergy; various pressure groups and fringe movements; youth groups; mission societies; clubs and societies – and so on.

If that's tedious to read, imagine how much more difficult it was to work with. It wasn't surprising that Carey dreamt of something simpler and more effective. What he and his advisers had in mind was a much clearer diagram with nice straight arrows all pointing inwards towards the archbishops.

Given the Church's resistance to change, this dream might not have been realized had it not been for a crisis which made change seem more urgent. In 1992, much to everyone's astonishment, the Church Commissioners supplied one.

'Unholy Saga of the Church's Missing Millions' said the headline in the *Financial Times*, which revealed that the Commissioners had lost the then enormous sum of 500 million pounds through risky speculation on property, supported by excessive borrowing. This was about as shocking as finding out that the rich maiden aunt on whom you have always relied for your monthly allowance and a fat legacy has lost everything in a drug-fuelled gambling spree.

Until then the Church Commissioners had seemed like the ultimate civil servants, as smooth and purring in their operation as a Rolls-Royce. A young female graduate who was employed there in Carey's time remembers being asked at her interview: 'If the angels said you could have more of any one particular virtue, which would you choose?' She replied, 'Patience', and got the job straight from university, working her way round various parts of No. 1 Millbank: 'Redundant churches, how can I help you?' Many of the Commissioners were still old school, including one whose office was filled with files stacked to the ceiling like ramparts. 'How do you cope?' the new recruit asked. 'Oh, I just chip away at it.'

Officially, the Commissioners included the archbishops, as well as delegates from each House in General Synod, but Geoffrey Fisher had been the first and last archbishop to take the role seriously. Carey delegated the task. In any case, it was the First Estates Commissioner and the Assets Committee who made the real investment decisions.

The Commissioners were part and parcel of the settlement of post-war Britain, intended to strengthen the Church as a national asset. They had an ethos of public service, and treated the Church and its leaders with the same sort of attitude as that shown to Jim Hacker by Sir Humphrey, the Permanent Secretary, in *Yes Minister*: the Commissioners were the sensible grown-ups, supporting the children's demands as much as they could, and coming over a bit stern when they couldn't. 'There is no pot of gold' became the famous mantra of the First Church Estates Commissioner as he addressed the General Synod's insatiable desire to spend.

In the 1960s and 70s, the Commissioners' investments performed spectacularly well. Fortune had smiled on them, because the portfolio they had inherited included great swathes of what was fast becoming prime real estate in London. And they had the funds to develop it. As planning restrictions lifted and the capital boomed, they entered into a series of highly lucrative deals with trusted property developers.

This satisfactory arrangement allowed the clergy to rise above material things. They could talk about poverty as much as they liked, without ever having to worry about experiencing it: the Commissioners were supplying the cash. In the boom years of the 1980s, as *Faith in the City* condemned shallow Thatcherite consumerism, the Commissioners were busy building large shopping malls like St Enoch's in Glasgow and the MetroCentre in Gateshead.

By the early 1990s, however, the portfolio had become dangerously tilted towards property. Some of the riskier developments failed at just the time that interest rates soared, property values came down, and Britain went into recession. The Commissioners were in trouble. A *Financial Times* journalist prodded about a bit and got an exclusive. It became national news. The senior Commissioners were hauled before Parliamentary and ecclesiastical committees to explain themselves, and church leaders assumed a stance of shocked innocence.

In truth, those leaders were partly to blame. In the spirit of welfare Britain, the Church had decided to set clergy stipends at the same level for everyone (except senior clergy). Whether they were young or old, fantastically successful or hopelessly inept, they would get the same deal. And that deal kept getting better. Stipends, pegged to those of teachers, rose annually. Vicarages were improved, their maintenance costs were covered, car loans were provided, expenses met, Council Tax paid, and generous retirement housing provision offered. The pension rose to guarantee two-thirds of a stipend – and clergy live a long time. To make it worse, Synod kept voting more and more people into the scheme: church bureaucrats, deaconesses, chaplains, staff of mission agencies, staff at theological colleges, and so on. Cathedrals were also wanting more money, as were dioceses. And so it went on. The Commissioners were paying.

In the end, the official enquiries uncovered recklessness, but no corruption. They did, however, find that there wasn't enough money to cover the by now enormous pensions liability. In order to fill that hole, the Commissioners had to make immediate and drastic cuts in spending. They stopped supporting almost everything except bishops, cathedrals and pensions. Cathedrals started to charge for entry, and dioceses had to raise money to pay their clergy and other staff. Rather than making cuts, they started to put the squeeze on people in the pew.

Although the Commissioners' assets recovered from the property speculation soon enough, the decisions instinctively taken in the aftermath set in motion a ratchet which would still further distance the Church from the England around it. The Commissioners had funded the Church as a whole. There was no financial link between the congregation and the incumbent. That's one reason why so much Anglican preaching is often dreadful – there's no penalty for dullness – but it has real advantages, too. But now the Church needed money, it turned instinctively to churchgoers, and to the committed, rather than to the occasional users, who might well have seen value in the buildings, or in the schools, and been prepared to pay for those, even if they had no desire to go to services.

What followed was a slow rebalancing of power. As bishops and dioceses became more self-sufficient, they started to flex their muscles a little more. Some of the richer parishes started to feel the same way: if they were now paying such large 'quotas' to the Church, why should they put up with things they didn't like? Hard-line evangelical ones threatened to stop paying, and some diverted their funds to other evangelicals. But most people sighed and dug deeper, and just about managed to satisfy the ever-growing demands from dioceses. Before the crisis, it was still quite common for people to fish around in their pockets and put some loose change into the collection plate, rather like leaving a small tip. A pound was normal. By 2014 people in the parishes would be donating over 900 million pounds per annum, around 70 per cent of the Church's annual income. But the power of the laity didn't increase accordingly. For them, it was taxation without representation.

For Carey the crisis couldn't have come at a better time. Not only did it add impetus to his drive for mission and evangelism; the Commissioners' failure allowed him to argue that a new Archbishops' Council was essential to coordinate the Church and improve oversight of its various parts.

By this point Carey had some heavyweight backers, mainly in the form of successful evangelical businessmen. A lot of the Archbishop of Canterbury's income-raising capacity had evaporated in Runcie's time when the Nikaean Club's reputation suffered after one of its members, Patrick Gilbert, was convicted of child abuse. (The Nikaean was a dining club, founded to encourage ecumenical relations, whose members paid for the opportunity to dine with the Archbishop of Canterbury and other senior clergy.)

Carey set about repairing the damage, and the 'Lambeth Partners', who had formerly done things like support the redevelopment of the Lambeth Palace gardens, were transformed into a much more serious group of financial backers and advisers.

The new central body they envisaged would be something like an old-fashioned telephone exchange. Its members would receive incoming messages from across the Church, consider them speedily, then route them to appropriate recipients. Congestion would be eased, crossed wires eliminated and nuisance callers blocked. The Church of England would emerge at last as an efficiently run organization equipped to meet the challenges of the new millennium.

The business of setting up this Council was long and complicated, and stretched over a great chunk of Carey's time in office. It was driven forward by those close to him, most publicly by Michael Turnbull, bishop of Durham, whose 1995 report *Working as One Body* spelled out its rationale.

Predictably, there was a great deal of criticism. Although they would all be represented on it, the separate fiefdoms of the Church feared that the real plan was to decapitate them and remove their autonomous decision-making powers. Bishops and deans were suspicious, since by sucking more power to itself, the Council could only weaken their power at diocesan and cathedral level. Clergy worried about central discipline being imposed on them. And most people worried about the creation of yet another layer of bureaucracy.

The image that was put forward to make the Council seem more attractive was that of a church tower with four pinnacles morphing into a single, thrusting church spire. The pinnacles were the four main power centres of the Church: the House of Bishops, the Commissioners, the General Synod and Church House. By being brought together on the Council under the leadership of the archbishops, they would be fused into a rational and efficient body working for the good of the Church as a whole.

The reason this rather contrived image never convinced was that the more obvious one which overlaid it was the executive board of a commercial company. As if to underline the point, a huge rugby-ball-shaped table sculpted from solid wood was commissioned. When it arrived, it turned out that it had the effect of blocking the sight-lines of everyone but the archbishops, so that members got cricks in their necks from craning to see who was speaking. It was quietly sold off after Carey left office.

In 1998 the Council finally came into being, legally established by the National Institutions Measure, a piece of legislation which managed to straighten out some other bits of the central church bureaucracy at the same time. Some of its early members still speak warmly about those first years, but find it hard to nail down what it achieved. The handful of outside members who weren't part of the central church establishment and considered themselves more in touch with the world were frustrated by the silence and caution with which their exciting new ideas were greeted. The forces of inertia were considerable: mutual suspicion between representatives of different church bodies, torn loyalties, nervousness about stepping out of line, and ambivalence about the whole enterprise.

Undaunted by this lack of enthusiasm, however, one new member organized a series of professional focus groups which canvassed churchgoers and non-churchgoers across the country to gauge their perceptions of the Church of England brand.

When asked to select images of people who personified the Church, under-twenty-fives chose Dame Thora Hird in an armchair, the Queen, and Cliff Richard. They also picked out images of 1950s Britain, and spoke about 'perfect families' with 'perfect children', a 'fantasy world' full of 'good people, who have no problems in life'. The Church, they opined, is 'constantly telling people what to do', and is 'scary'. One selected the picture of a lion: 'It waits until you're just beginning to feel relaxed and comfortable, and then it pounces on you and rips you apart – saying how bad you are.'

For their 'mood boards', one youth cut out a picture of a table formally laid for dinner and stuck across it the caption 'Control yourself'. Another juxtaposed a picture of George Carey heading a football with a dinosaur wearing a casual outfit, explaining that while the Church likes to look trendy, it's only skin deep. A picture of an oil rig in the North Sea miles from the mainland and a lonely dolphin conveyed the idea that 'The Church of England is all alone and has little contact with the rest of the world', and pictures of a desert and a snowscape stretching to the horizon with the caption 'ETERNITY' stuck across them were used to underline the point that 'The services are boring and go on and on.'

The Archbishops' Council received these findings in silence. They'd never been keen on the project, and now they knew why. 'Thank you for your work,' said Carey, 'but I'm afraid you've spoken to the wrong people.'

Although it strengthened the archbishops' power, and made some 'efficiency gains', the Council did not address any of the real weaknesses of the Church. After the focus group experiment, it declined to establish any serious way of receiving signals from Blair's Britain. It pumped up the motor part of the Church's nervous system without noticing that the sensory part was missing. It failed to make serious cuts or savings, merely adding another large blob to the organogram and another committee to service. 'It could fairly be said to represent nothing except itself', concluded the historian Andrew Chandler. In the long term it had the dangerous effect of encouraging small groups of leaders to meet in the shadows to make far-reaching decisions without consulting other parts of the Church.

Carey was out of his depth. He genuinely believed that fiddling with a few levers in a simulated cockpit was going to pull the Church out of its tailspin. 'Reaction [to the Archbishop's Council] was generally positive,' he concluded in his memoirs, 'although I was amazed that some chose to call it "bureaucratic"'.

He took refuge in his supposed role as a world statesman, touring the Anglican Communion and bringing back more palatable messages from more attractive young people in other lands. Ysenda Maxtone Graham recounts a frustrating year spent trying unsuccessfully to arrange an interview with him to inform the book she was writing about the Church of England. When she eventually managed to corner John Habgood and ask why the archbishops were so busy, he explained that they were keeping in touch with the world Church so that the English Church knew the context in which it was making decisions. '"I've just seen the Archbishop of Canterbury's diary for 1993," he smiled, "and was almost asking, "When's he going to be in England?" "Are your journeys really necessary?"', she asked with some irritation. 'He didn't laugh.'

This kind of self-deception undermined Carey's otherwise straightforward approach, and ultimately his time in office. It was under his leadership that the disastrous 'Lambeth 1.10' resolution on homosexuality was passed in 1998 (the subject of a later chapter); well before that, however, in 1991 the House of Bishops published the report *Issues in Human Sexuality*, suppressing the more thoughtful and honest report which had been prepared by a committee drawn from all factions of the Church and chaired by June Osborne before Tony Higton spooked the horses. Despite Carey's reassurance that *Issues* was not 'the last word on the subject', it was quickly adopted as official policy. It said that laypeople could enter into monogamous homosexual relationships if they really must, but clergy couldn't. There was nothing sinful about homosexual 'orientation' per se, but 'genital acts' fall short of the standard required of the clergy.

This was a compromise at best, moralistic clericalism at worst. Even apart from the whole issue of whether homosexuality was wrong, it assumed that clergy were distinguished from laity by virtue of their greater moral purity, a view which clashed both with common sense and with the traditional view that it is God's grace rather than clerical sanctity which makes the Church's sacraments efficacious. It was also hypocritical, for it pretended that clergy were less likely to have gay sex than the rest of the population, when most people in the Church thought that the opposite was the case – not least in relation to some of the bishops who signed off the document.

This sort of dishonesty did enormous damage. A broad church like the Church of England had always had to accommodate a diversity of views, even around deeply held moral convictions. In the past, right up until the time of Carey, it had done so by the policy of 'don't ask, don't tell'. That was how society used to operate as well. But since the 1960s this had become increasingly untenable. Not only had Britain become far more diverse in its beliefs and values than in the past, it had been moving steadily towards a culture of greater openness and 'transparency'.

In the early 1990s the Blair government legislated to guarantee individuals access to their personal information, and to open up the inner workings of public bodies. Managerialism in the Church might not have been such a bad thing if it had meant the adoption of the same standards as those accepted by the rest of the public sector, but the CofE managed to exempt itself from things like the Freedom of Information Act by arguing that it was different and normal public standards did not apply. It also evaded the more attractive aspects of the private sector, like a willingness to cut costs, a more entrepreneurial spirit, attentiveness to the views of your customers, performance review, and devolution of power from the centre.

Instead, the Church under Carey took refuge in a managerial voodoo. Like a cargo cult, it assumed that if you aped the jargon and waved some of the symbols, success and prestige must naturally follow. It didn't. At the start of the Decade of Evangelism, usual Sunday attendance in the Church of England was 969,000. By its close, it had fallen to 810,400, despite the growth of the overall population. Church attendance and affiliation were in freefall.

Carey and the bishops had backed themselves into a corner. They knew they couldn't go on with the culture of a nod and a wink, but neither were they willing to embrace openness and honesty and admit the Church's diversity, humanity and fallibility. They took refuge in make-believe. The attempt to make the Church into a centrally managed organization produced something imposing in its sheer incongruity, like a hotel carved from blocks of ice. But they had built their ice palace not on land, but on the river from which the ice was cut. The currents underneath were destroying its foundations.

# 7

# Charismatic signs and wonders

The most astonishing development in twentieth-century Christianity came like a thief in the night, and those who watched only the brightly lit and public parts of religion saw nothing at all out of order until half of the fixtures had silently disappeared. In their place came noises: singing, laughing, long, burbling flows of nonsense syllables, shouts, giggles and sometimes animal sounds; but the noise in which Andrew first heard the change was a series of four heavy thuds, followed by a sudden rapid drumming – like the noise that rabbits make to warn one another – when people started to shake uncontrollably and beat their feet against the floor.

The laughter was the strangest thing. From three or four places in the church you could hear this gut-busting abandoned giggle. It was not an adult sound at all. It was more like the laughter that you get by tickling a happy toddler; but it was coming from respectable women in their thirties. They sounded as if they had just been told the best joke in the world and it was going on and on and on …

All around, the same thing was happening to other members of the congregation, but even more astonishingly the people who remained upright did not seem disconcerted at all. They just kept praying in English, or murmuring long, glistening streams of nonsense. They were used to their fellows fainting. It was just the Holy Spirit at work. A tanned blonde in a blue dress, who had been prayed over for about ten minutes, suddenly went down sideways across a line of plastic chairs. She was helped to the floor, where she wept with heart-rending abandon. A single string of pearls showed in her newly washed hair. She curled on her side and sobbed while two women helpers knelt beside her with their hands on her back, praying quietly.

Slowly her weeping died away. There was another burst of drumming on the floor, but this was just a rush of children released from the crèche part of the service. They ran down the side of the church, apparently taking no notice of what was going on, and rejoined their parents at the back. This was, after all, an Anglican church in the heart of South Kensington, with a well-heeled congregation that had put nearly four thousand pounds into the collection bag the previous Sunday for Rwandan relief. If people were going to faint, shake and laugh like drunks, this was no excuse for staring.

It had taken nearly seventy years for the charismatic revival to reach the English upper classes from its first appearance in modern times at the start of the twentieth century among poor and marginalized groups – a black congregation in Los Angeles in 1906, chapels in Wales, followers of women healers in China. In affluent London they had deliberately prayed for these manifestations for months, convinced that God would reward them as he had rewarded the earliest Christians with supernatural gifts of prophecy, healing and understanding, all expressed in an unknown language. All these are clearly described in the Acts of the Apostles and in Paul's letters, and had appeared sporadically throughout Christian history, but they seem to have been almost unknown from the first century until sometime after the Reformation. There is a subterranean record of glossolalia which, according to Sarah Coakley, '[gives] the lie to the suspicion that this gift has been totally dormant since the apostolic age', but it is hard to track. After the Reformation a few sparks had landed in sectarian groups, often obscure sects widely derided as crazy or dangerous. There were more respectable versions too. In Britain one of them, the Catholic Apostolic Church, had gained a foothold in Victorian high society. Fainting, or falling in the power of the Spirit, was much more common than glossolalia, but it could be downplayed as simply a sign of great emotion.

There were working-class Pentecostal communities in Wales and in Lancashire, among other places, by the mid-1960s, but it was during the 1970s that the charismatic revival burgeoned and the movement began to spread into the mainstream denominations. When it did so it seemed to make denominational boundaries wholly irrelevant. They were not. It's very notable that the movement seems to have broken into the Church of England from America, rather than from among the British working class where it had existed for decades. The General Synod first noticed the phenomenon in 1978. By that time, though, some evangelical leaders had realized it could be just the thing to give evangelicalism the popular appeal it had so far lacked.

The early charismatics were marked above all by spontaneity and unexpectedness. As the movement grew, it became more formalized, more theological, and routinized. It allied itself increasingly with evangelicalism, taking over its conservative sexual ethics, gender attitudes and close connections with the English class system. In this it resembled what happened to the LSD-soaked culture of the American West Coast, which fed into it through the 'Jesus Freaks'. The early groups were small, informal and exploratory. A house group might sing for fifteen or twenty minutes until one of the leaders began singing in tongues, and then everyone would. The experience was one of huge relief and freedom. Again and again the language used came back to water, to springs and to refreshment. Women and young people found their voices. There were no clergy. The Spirit itself was conceived of as moving in waves, and these waves were rushing back up Dover Beach. The more cerebral and straight-laced evangelicals saw what was happening, and some realized that they might be able to reach out, especially to young people, in a way they had largely failed to do since the war. The 'square' might be able to become a bit more 'hip'.

By the time the General Synod noticed the phenomenon, another Cambridge-educated public school evangelical, David Watson, had become the leading figure. Watson was associated particularly with healing miracles. His church in York, St Michael le Belfrey, became a kind of pilgrimage shrine, and when he was diagnosed with liver cancer he confidently expected that God would heal him from this, too. So did his followers. But he died anyway, in 1984.

The movement recuperated, and rallied around the American evangelist and musician John Wimber, who had become a hugely important figure in English Christianity, though one quite under the radar of most religious coverage. Wimber repackaged evangelical fervour in a Californian soft-rock package. There was already an English alternative – 'house churches' had grown spontaneously from Baptist and Brethren roots around charismatic leaders such as Terry Virgo and Gerald Coates and combined into loose networks; but the Californian version was more sensually overwhelming and less authoritarian. Wimber's performances followed a strict pattern: twenty minutes to half an hour of emotional community singing: simple, repetitive lyrics full of longing sung to a pulsing beat with overarching washes of heavenly sounds. Then a 'teaching sermon' designed to shake the mind loose from twentieth-century assumptions about rationality and science, and to move back into a timelessness where the miracles of the Bible could be expected immediately. Finally a time of 'ministry' and healing when the Pentecostal gifts were to be made manifest.

The transformation from the cool and static grandeur of Prayer Book Anglicanism was complete.

Before then, another emotional impulse revivifying evangelicalism had also come from America, but in a very different form, one doctrinally completely opposed to the charismatic revival: the crusades of Billy Graham. These shaped an entire generation of Anglican evangelicals – but not because they made converts. In a pattern that was to become familiar, the effect of the big stadium meetings that Graham brought to Britain was much stronger among the already converted than among their notional targets. Graham's crusades were theatrical, which meant that they involved both organization and emotion on a scale far beyond the ambitions of a parish church. He could draw 50,000 people to Wembley Stadium, over a period of weeks. This demanded organization and generated emotion on a scale that only royal occasions could otherwise generate within the established church. Nor did the organization stop when the doors closed. There was a system of follow-up visits, and everyone who came up to the altar to announce they had been converted was meant to be followed up by their parish church.

Whether there were many such converts from among the spectators was another matter. Wembley Stadium found that its future lay in football matches rather than evangelical shows. But the Graham 'Crusades' changed the lives of a generation of aspiring English evangelical young men. What typically happened was that a serious young layman spent months or weeks volunteering in the administration of these events and found this work was more congenial and far more rewarding than whatever he had been doing outside. So off he went to get ordained, full of hope and heroics, a style epitomized even forty years later by Justin Welby's remark as bishop of Durham, when he looked around a diocese where church attendance had fallen by a third in fifteen years, and said that there were probably as many active Christians there as there had been in St Cuthbert's day in the seventh century – and look what Cuthbert had achieved!

The other long-term significance of the Graham movement was that it legitimized mass emotion as an element of upper-class English Christianity and so prepared the way for the charismatic influence. The appeal to feeling was still widely felt to be wrong or illegitimate: the evangelical movement still understood itself as a rational and intellectual one. But in practice an element of something close to ecstasy was starting to be admitted to a place that had been very dry and stony. This didn't happen without friction. One of the earliest and most influential charismatics in the Church of England, Michael Harper, left his job as John Stott's curate in 1964 after Stott decided he was being carried away by his enthusiasms. Stott wanted the whole of England converted, while the charismatic movement operated in a piecemeal and unpredictable way, bubbling up from local enthusiasms. Besides, the emotional element was repugnant in a culture which relied on reason and moral order to tame the passions. But elsewhere in the movement men of similar background saw opportunity, and some found they could surrender their hearts and be renewed.

Sandy Millar, an Etonian barrister from a Scottish Presbyterian background, would have seemed a natural for Stott's brand of evangelicalism. But at some stage in the early 1970s, his girlfriend took him to hear an American preacher, David du Plessis, at the Baptist Metropolitan Tabernacle in south London, and du Plessis brought with him the techniques of the charismatic revival and prayed that these gifts might be shared with those who wanted them.

Later that night, Millar started praying in tongues, and he has never stopped since. In 1976 he was installed as the curate in Holy Trinity Brompton, then a society church in Kensington. There he started – with the vicar's blessing – to experiment in small groups with the invocation of the Holy Spirit. The interesting thing about this is that it quite often works. Charismatic manifestations are quite inarguable, especially the glossolalia, so characteristic of the charismatic revival. What they mean can be wrangled about, but the behaviours themselves cannot be gainsaid, forgotten or explained away. What is even odder is that if small, determined groups of people pray and prepare for supernatural manifestations, these may well appear. Mass hysteria fits more comfortably into the known scheme of things: a full-on Pentecostal roadshow is quite like a Grateful Dead concert in terms of deliberate and cultivated derangement of the senses; but what developed in churches like Holy Trinity Brompton (now known as 'HTB') were small, polite and English ways to make reality squirm, miracles performed on chintz sofas.

Andrew's one experience of this kind of thing was oddly low key, though it came at a time of great emotional tension. He was in Bosnia, about fifteen miles from the front line of the war, but sheltered in cowardice and ignorance because he was accompanying a party of working-class Catholic pilgrims to the shrine of the Virgin at Medjugorje, where she is supposed to have appeared daily to a group of village children. Medjugorje and the surrounding villages were the scenes of atrocity during the Second World War; one day Andrew was driven to a Franciscan monastery set on a strategic hilltop where in 1943 an energetic Catholic had been presented with a suckling pig in the great hall for cutting the throats of more than a thousand 'schismatics' or Serbian Orthodox prisoners. As the coach drew up, the guide praised the bravery of the defenders who had been overwhelmed when the communist partisans captured the place in 1945.

His fellow pilgrims were under the impression that the monks had been fighting against the Nazis rather than as their enthusiastic allies, but the complexities of history were more alive to Andrew. He felt extremely lonely. The group listened to a wonderful theatrical sermon about the atrocities committed by 'the Turks', or Muslim Bosnians, and the woman next to him grabbed his hand and started praying in tongues with as little drama as if she were reading from a shopping list. He felt nothing but embarrassment and some curiosity, so when she led him to the communion rails to receive a blessing, he went along. The priest looked him in the eye, and made some gesture – he forgets what – and perhaps five minutes later, as he stood quietly in a courtyard, he felt suddenly wrapped in a bubble of slippery joy. It was a bit like being sunstruck, although with an added component of inexplicable benevolence towards his fellow creatures. Despite the extreme unprofessionalism of such a sentiment, it took a very long time to wear off.

Many years later, after Millar had become the rector of HTB, Andrew got to watch his technique at close quarters, on a trip around Romania shortly after the Iron Curtain fell. It was a journey in which entirely different periods of history were crushed together like the layers in puff pastry. BMWs drove at homicidal speeds down roads where you might also meet a shepherd driving his flock, wearing the skin of a less fortunate sheep. This region had been one of the first places where the Reformation took root in Europe, and now it was taking root again, and spreading eastwards, across Romania to the Ukraine and Russia itself. The party delivered computer equipment to a wooden house in a small Transylvanian town, but to reach the front door from their car they had to step over a gutter which was running with blood from the pig that had been slaughtered in the road by a neighbour up the hill.

Much of Transylvania had been largely German speaking until the ethnic cleansings of the twentieth century and still concealed a vigorous Calvinist church network, mostly for the ethnic Hungarians. Indeed, it had been an ethnic Hungarian pastor, Laszlo Tökes, who had sparked off the final revolution against Ceauşescu with his sermons in Timişoara the previous winter.

Millar was accompanied by a couple of strapping young acolytes fresh out of public school filled with beaming, beefy confidence. The three of them visited a Baptist school in Oradea, where they put on a show designed to evangelize the English upper-middle classes: testimony – 'My mother is a Christian and my father is not. I grew up believing, and at the age of six I asked Jesus to be my lord. It was a very simple thing to do,' said Jezza (or James), and James (or was it Jezza?) reassured the children: 'It is very easy to think that your testimony is not worthwhile if you have not been into sin and sex and drugs.'

'Just recently I have been struck with how incredible it is to have a personal relationship with the creator of the universe,' said Jamie, the intellectual one. The students were politely baffled by Sandy Millar's banter about cricket and 'soccer' and rugger and Scotland, none of which they appeared to have heard of.

At the end, Sandy taught them a song. It went, all of it:

I'll say yes yes yes
I'll say yes yes yes
I'll say yes Lord
I'll say yes Lord
I'll say yes yes yes.

The tune was more complicated.

Sandy said afterwards it was wonderful that the children only needed one repetition to learn it.

Later Jezza (or James), being nice, recoiled with horror from a Romanian pimp who approached him in the hotel lobby, offered him first a girl and, when she was declined, proposed a boy instead.

The guide to the party was entirely different: a middle-aged Essex man, straightforward and compassionate, who had been smuggling Bibles and nurturing underground Christian networks for decades, ducking and diving for Jesus. Andrew liked him immensely and respected his skill with authorities. 'I'm a fundamentalist, of course,' he said at one stage while they drove through the Transylvanian mountains, and so they sparred a little about evolution. But in his world, to be a fundamentalist was a simple marker of decency. Millar's expedition got its ground troops a long way from Windsor Castle. HTB is unselfconsciously posh and very wealthy, but it isn't snobbish – or at least it is not entirely comfortable with snobbery, and that's an important distinction.

Millar stayed almost entirely in the background for the visit. He was always Etonian. Shrewd, slippery, polite of course, but beyond that profoundly courteous and self-deprecating, with a great capacity for consideration of others, and a will of iron behind the twinkling bonhomie. When he was asked to talk at one of the churches, he spoke as modestly as possible, in a low-key way suggesting that they pray for the Holy Spirit. This was of course a major incursion across a theological front line: the evangelicals he talked to were opposed to the charismatic revival on biblical grounds, just as Stott and his church had been. But he spoke with such calm and politeness that it seemed an entirely reasonable and harmless suggestion. The other thing to emerge from that little encounter was the boundless confidence of these men that God was working closely with them, and that if these suspicious Romanians were to pray as he suggested, the Holy Spirit would astonish them.

In that sense, HTB really was full of a kind of faith while the rest of the Church of England wavered. It viewed the subtleties of men like David Jenkins or Don Cupitt or even Robert Runcie as equivocation.

This trust in the future was only reinforced in 1994 when the Toronto Blessing – the most exuberant manifestation of the charismatic revival – came to London and started to manifest itself in the way described at the beginning of the chapter.

The point about highly emotional religion is that its intensity quickly subsides and has to be revived by some other novelty. The phenomenon of being 'slain in the Spirit' so that one falls over and lies on the floor in a semi-conscious state had reached Kendal in Cumbria, where Linda encountered it, by 1995. Seated expectantly after a good dose of singing and preaching, anticipation was high by the time the visiting preacher from America called people forward.  Orderly queues formed as people waited politely to get to the front. Catchers were conveniently stationed to smooth the descent to the floor. As the preacher's hand pressed on each head in a physically forceful blessing, it was virtually obligatory to fall backwards into the waiting arms. Whether pushed or slain was never entirely clear.

The whole episode is now shrouded in some embarrassment but it contributed to an atmosphere of millennial expectation which was quite general among evangelicals in the middle of that decade. Nicky Lee, who led the service at St Paul's, Onslow Square, that Andrew watched, said when they talked afterwards, 'I hope that it will go on and on until the Lord returns' and Andrew had the distinct impression he thought that would be in his lifetime.

A very strange group of Americans known as the Kansas City Prophets were also taken up by HTB at around this time. One was housed in a basement office at the church for some months. Yet HTB withstood the shock when the prophets turned out to be embarrassingly crazy and the return of Jesus was once more delayed. There is a streak of cold-blooded pragmatism that runs through the organization and informs its strategy. This is common across all the manifestations of what Rob Warner labels 'entrepreneurial evangelicalism'.

The charismatic experience felt from the inside like a wave, something coherent and irresistible in its liquid power. But as its latest phase of enthusiasm rushed again and again against the shingles of Dover Beach it broke, as waves must, into fragments and eddies.

The first and most obvious division was between the 'charismatic evangelicals', as they had now become, and the rest of the Church. The experience had the paradoxical effect of heightening feelings of brotherhood and belonging across denominational or theological boundaries *and* sharpening divisions within them. The shared bliss of praying in tongues could draw together Catholics and Protestants as nothing else could. At the same time, the experience was inaccessible and rather off-putting to those outside it and it often led to a new form of snobbery, in which those people who did not have it or want it were regarded as inferior or less Christian than those who did.

In the wider evangelical movement there was, and remains, a clear division between the traditional Protestants – for whom these manifestations were something between frippery and delusion compared to the solid assurance of biblical truth manifest in moral lives, since the power to work and experience miracles had ended with apostolic time – and those who embraced it: between John Stott and Sandy Millar, or conservative Baptists and the Vineyard churches. This split played out at different scales, fractally, throughout Western Christianity, often within congregations, as happened with Tony Higton's in Essex. It seems to have been divisive even in St Paul's time, to judge from his letters.

Such divisions weakened the movement, as did the inevitable waning of charismatic spirit. The history of religious movements shows that it is relatively easy to found new churches and generate enormous rates of growth. The difficulty is to sustain them beyond the first generation – if that. Schisms can close churches within a decade of their founding, and often did in the case of small charismatic ones. The 'myth of evangelical growth' did not last much beyond the end of the twentieth century – except in the minds of those who were still willing it to be true. But charismatic evangelical Anglicanism had two real and lasting successes.

The first concerned young people, especially students. There is something particularly appealing and comforting about evangelicalism for some people at this stage of life. Nearly every university town can boast a flourishing evangelical church with a rotating door of students. Some, particularly young men, would be sufficiently touched by the experience to offer themselves for ordination like their Billy Graham-inspired predecessors.

The second lasting success was among circles of affluent 'home counties' English middle classes. Generally speaking the movement does not translate into rural areas – there the arrival of a 'happy clappy' vicar is often a disaster for all parties. But most towns and cities can sustain at least one successful and lively evangelical church aimed at families. Of these new middle-class parishes, HTB and its offshoots would prove to be the most important.

As the charismatic movement continued, further divisions appeared within it. Was the experience one to be constantly repeated? How Christian could you be if it never happened to you? Sarah Coakley recorded such tensions in two churches in Lancaster, where the Anglican congregation had actually split in the ten years since the gifts of the Spirit first appeared, not between charismatics and those who rejected the new, but between more or less charismatic believers. The Anglicans withdrew from the public use of tongues in their services 'after some episodes which were felt to be excessive and unedifying', although the congregation would still sometimes break out in communal singing, which was acceptable if unplanned. People were encouraged to use tongues in private prayer, but the public babble was 'somewhat repetitive and trite'. By contrast, the more evangelical group that had split off felt that theatrical demonstrations were an important witness to unbelievers and potential converts.

Andrew has had it seriously explained that the reason God does not resurrect the dead at English ecclesiastical events the way that frequently happens in Africa (if we are to judge by the evidence of evangelical DVDs) is simply that the English don't have enough faith. So there are plenty of Anglican charismatics who have had their reasoning faculties quite pureed by the Holy Spirit until they attained the happy blank credulity of acid casualties.

Some heavily charismatic congregations like St Andrew's Chorleywood more or less levitated out of the Church of England altogether and subsisted in their own orbit. Bishop David Pytches, a leader in this congregation, is the author of a little book called *Does God Speak Today?* in which he recounts such miracles as the Holy Spirit showing John Wimber a glowing red 'A' above the head of a woman travelling on the same flight as him to reveal that she was an adulteress. Graham Dow, who became bishop of Carlisle, once told Andrew with the glee of the justified that 'there are no atheists in cancer wards'. He also published a little booklet on deliverance, from which it appears that homoeopathy, acupuncture and oral sex can all let demons into your life. That anal sex allows the evil spirits to wriggle past your haemorrhoids probably goes without saying. Dow became briefly famous for suggesting that the floods of 2007 were God's commentary on same-sex marriage.

But at HTB they kept a lid on these excesses. This didn't entirely prevent the rest of the Church of England from regarding them as dangerous weirdos: a curate's wife who went on an Alpha course there in the mid-1990s has a story about how her group left the building and found there were no buses running. So they formed a prayer circle on the pavement of the Brompton Road to summon a bus. A bus turned up, perhaps in answer to their prayers, but by this time the circle was so much fun that they just kept on praying.

The driver slowed down, saw a group of people who clearly had no interest in his services, and pulled away again without stopping.

Yet at least people came out of charismatic churches like HTB in South Kensington fired up to do something, however pointless. What made HTB uniquely successful were not just the advantages of geographical and social position, as a central London church for the new English ruling class, but the way these were exploited with organization, ambition and political skill. In the Alpha Course, it had also found a global product which was quickly winning a market share among the rapidly growing ranks of the entrepreneurial global middle classes.

Within HTB and the evangelical movement generally, there was a growing frustration with 'liberals' all through this period, which had roots in far more practical things than theology. One major conflict was over church planting: the practice of taking over failing church buildings with a seed congregation of believers from a successful church. This was and remains absolutely central to HTB's project. In fact St Paul's, Onslow Square, where Andrew watched the Toronto Blessing, was an HTB plant. So is St Mark's, Battersea Rise, a church in Clapham planted when central London became impossible for HTB's traditional congregants to afford and they started to buy houses south of the river. All in all there are at least twenty HTB church plants across London. Most have been successful, numerically and especially financially. None the less, the total congregations of HTB and all its church plants across London do not exceed 12,000 after thirty years of effort. It's not a miracle cure. But to those on the inside the church plant serves as a validation of what they're doing, since, of course, the church flourishes because

God is pleased with HTB. It is also important precisely because it demands enormous commitment from the planters, who are taking on a really difficult and time-consuming project.

Since the Church has a huge overstock of the kind of draughty Victorian barns that HTB plants into, and the process normally transforms them into popular centres of community and worship, it's hard to see why the process arouses such hostility among outsiders. There is at least one bad reason, and two good ones. The bad reason is – mostly – jealousy. In the Church of England, for all the period since 1986, the progress of numerical decline has been undeniable, however frantically denied. Everyone who works within it knows their congregations are getting smaller and older, and their concerns further and further removed from those of the world around them. So it is extremely irritating to have a bunch of smug, shiny young people claiming that they know the answer, and that – furthermore – God loves what they are doing, with the implication that He is displeased with those parts of the Church which aren't growing.

This irritation is sometimes, more respectably, stated in theological terms. The Calvinist roots of the HTB movement are still present in the Alpha Course. The rebarbative doctrine of penal substitutionary atonement and a sexual ethic built around an idealized version of the nuclear family seem to many Christians both theologically and ethically objectionable. The belief in worldly success as a sign of God's blessing also appears a contradiction of the gospel. Against this, a defender of HTB might argue that the Calvinist teachings of the original Alpha Course have been lost or diluted as it succeeds more widely. To an outsider, that appears uncontroversially true. You need only look at successive editions of the Alpha material to see the process in action – a gradual softening on homosexuality for example. But that isn't a defence that anyone inside HTB can make, nor, possibly, one they can even allow themselves to formulate. It is an important part of evangelical self-image to suppose that they are successful, and liberal churches fail, because God is pleased by evangelical worship and that – though compelled by His nature to love all, even liberals – He loves the liberals with a bored distaste.

Most importantly, there is a sense in which the central secret of HTB's success threatens some of the foundations of the Church of England. Church planting works, in the sense that it makes some new congregations. But it does so at the expense of the idea that the Church of England is a church for everyone, and that it is best as a broad church in which diversity is respected. The theory of church planting, developed at the Fuller Seminary in California, and whole-heartedly embraced by HTB, is based on affinity marketing. People catch religion from people like them. Strange beliefs become reasonable when they are espoused by people like us, whose reasonable character we trust in other contexts.

In practice, the Church of England had always worked like every other institution, within a network of affinities. But they were broader, more diverse, and with more influential roles available to women, single people and other marginals – at least in terms of informal leadership. And in its self-image, at least, it had been a church for everyone. This remains the rhetoric of many evangelical churches even – perhaps especially – when they are most socially distinct from the world around them. Only the full-on Calvinists, with their comforting certainty that almost everyone is damned, could not feel this obligation.

Sociologists distinguish between churches that work in the market, finding their own distinctive social niches like HTB, competing with others and rewarding their customers, and those that work as a kind of public utility, supplying services to everyone indifferently. It had been the case for almost all the twentieth century – strengthened by a universal welfare ethos – that the Church of England had seen its status as a public utility as one of the most important things about it. But all of the new and vigorous currents in evangelical Christianity rejected this understanding. If the souls of outsiders were to benefit from Christianity, this could only be by being converted, not merely by being baptized, or married, or even buried. Some of the spokesmen of HTB were quite explicit about their intentions. The old Church of England had failed, but it was a useful container for them to occupy and turn to a more profitable purpose. England meant little to them; it was winning the world for Jesus which excited them, and the global Anglican Church seemed like a good place to start.

In terms of our theoretical three-legged stool, the belief leg – which serves to differentiate rather than unite true believers from others – became more important, and the everyday custom and practice element of religion was downplayed or derided. The faithful women and men who still came to church every week because it was 'just what you do' were starting to be viewed as lukewarm or worse. A 'personal relationship with Jesus' and a ready ability to spell out one's belief in neat propositions and selected biblical verses gained currency. On this point both the charismatics and the old, stiff evangelicals were as one.

This process may have been inevitable and it was certainly self-reinforcing. The further that England drifted from the Church of England, the more it required a deliberate leap to move between them: not just a leap of faith, but one of social positioning as well. In 1986 it would have been – it was in fact – remarkable for a bishop to have had a conversion experience though, curiously, the two men most hated by the evangelical party, Habgood and Jenkins, had both had such experiences in their late teens. But even in those cases, what happened was an assent to something which had always seemed reasonable and potentially true, just not very urgent. Most bishops had simply grown up Christian. They didn't need to be converted any more than they needed to be told to drive on the left. By 2016 this was not true at all. Most bishops had had identifiable conversions. They had not grown up as Christians. This might be the result of a bias in the selection process towards evangelicals, and perhaps there was an element of that. But it also and more importantly reflected the way in which Christians generally were becoming more self-conscious about their beliefs and their identity, more at odds with the rest of England.

# 8

# Dreams of a global church

Part of the way in which self-conscious Christians felt set apart from what they viewed as an increasingly secular England was through their sense of belonging to a movement that transcended nationality. For some Anglican clergy, this found expression in a belief in the reality of the Anglican Communion; but there were profoundly destructive currents moving there as well. The American culture wars and the post-colonial resentments of sub-Saharan Africa came together in a fight about homosexuality – but also about miracles, about patriarchy, and about power and authority – which blew the whole show apart and was immensely damaging to the Church of England too. The centrepiece was the Lambeth Conference of 1998, a three-week gathering of all the Anglican bishops in the world at the campus of the University of Kent, on a hill overlooking Canterbury Cathedral.

Approaching the great schism George Carey's staff were cheerful in the way you sometimes find in the wives of alcoholics and philanderers. In doomed organizations, this is called leadership. One of Dr Carey's staff said to Andrew before the Conference: 'All those who take part are going to say, one way or another, "Archbishop, this has been the most incredible experience of my life!"' Andrew must have looked doubtful even down the telephone, for after a pause she explained: 'But the experience will be in their souls and psyches. It won't come out of the documents. People in outward ways will be crucified.'

The Lambeth Conference of 1998 started – and might as well have ended – with a fine piece of theatre. On a sunny day, outside the sports hall of the University of Kent where the Conference was held, a couple of decrepit white bishops held up a banner demanding an 'inclusive church'. They were both gay, but had only managed to come out after their wives had died and they had already endured lifetimes of episcopal respectability. About thirty yards away the bishop of Enugu, in Nigeria, was shouting at Richard Kirker, the general secretary of the Lesbian and Gay Christian Movement: 'God himself has condemned homosexuality in the Scriptures; and Scripture is the base for the faith of Christians. So if you are a Christian, why not go to what the Scripture says about gay' – he mashed out the vowel of the word like a savoury curse – 'and about homosexuality? This issue was in the early church and it was addressed in First Corinthians, chapter 6, verses 9–10.'

The bishop held his floppy, black-eared Bible in front of his chest, pushing stubby fingers across the page. 'Romans chapter 1, verse 27 says even those who support homosexuals and those who are involved in it – in lustful carnality of man with man – will be punished!' By now there was a ring of spectators around them. A television crew had pushed to the front and both men raised their voices to be heard more clearly by the reporters at the back.

'Look at the Old Testament! There in Leviticus it says those boys should be stoned to death. And also – Genesis, chapter 2 ...' As the bishop scrabbled through his Bible, Kirker managed a word in edgeways: 'Would you be prepared to stone us to death?' It didn't sound a wholly rhetorical question in the treacly heat. He was a deacon, who had made it to within six months of the priesthood before his lover, another priest, was killed in a motorcycle accident; and in his grief he had said things which made it impossible for his bishop to ordain him. It did not matter that he was gay. But he refused to dissemble or to regret his sex life. So he had spent the subsequent twenty years campaigning for acceptance of gay people in the Church, and in this task seemed to have discovered a vocation.

Facing the bishop, Kirker looked birdlike, as if a gust of wind could blow him away. But he had the tenacity of a finch clinging with both feet to a swaying tree. 'Would you be prepared to stone us to death?' Kirker asked again.

The bishop pushed on with undiminished force: 'Because of the grace of Christ, you would be counselled; you would be prayed for.' His manner left no doubt that the justice of God demanded stoning, even if His mercy prescribed no more than exorcism: '... and you would be delivered out of your homosexuality. And I'm going to lay my hands on you and deliver you to become a total and dedicated Christian.'

He reached forward to touch Kirker's sandy, neatly bristled hair. 'I lay my hands on you in the name of the Lord! Father, in the name of Jesus, I lay my hand on him!' The bishop's wife, paler, shorter, with her hair in long braids, began a steady, melodic chant of alleluia, alleluia, alleluia, which continued for a while underneath the hoarser shouting of the contending men.

'Father, I tell you in the name of JESUS, deliver him.'

Kirker tried pushing the hand away. The bishop pressed it down and shouted louder: 'I can deliver you! God wants to deliver you! In the name of JESUS! Father, I pray that you deliver him from homosexuality in the name of JESUS! Father, I deliver him out of homosexuality, out of gay! That he become a Christian! A genuine Christian! A devoted Christian! In the name of Jesus! Alleluia! Alleluia! Alleluia!' His wife panted along with him, 'alleluia, alleluia', as they descended from the climax of their ritual.

There is always something deeply sexual about Pentecostal religion even at its most fraudulent: the effort, the ecstasy, the concentration. But this was Pentecostalism without the props. There was no organ, no darkness from which the audience could gaze at a lit stage, no one waiting for a miracle. Instead, there was a ring of journalists, and some of them started to giggle. This was partly because of the tall and unfeasibly handsome blond from a television company who kept trying to get a story he could understand. He pushed his microphone between the two men and asked, 'Gentlemen, do you think there is any room for compromise on this issue?'

Kirker confessed to a failed heterosexual relationship. 'I want Jesus to change you!' cried the bishop. 'You said you tried to be – to marry. You couldn't sustain it. Why don't you try again?' Then Kirker announced that he had been born and grown up in Nigeria, quite close to Enugu. For a flicker of a moment there seemed to be some possibility of human contact. The bishop stopped looking at him as if he were a bird-headed demon, fouling the ground he stood on. But at that moment Kirker pecked. 'And I had my first sexual experience with a Nigerian boy!' The bishop shouted as if he had been struck in the eye. 'No!' Kirker put his head on one side and pecked again. 'That proves it is nonsense to say there is no homosexuality in Africa.' Shouting like Samson in agony, the bishop cried: 'You brought it with you!' – and the ring of spectators collapsed in laughter.

That evening Chukwuma and Kirker were taken to London in separate limousines to repeat their argument in three different television studios. With that theatrical performance, the possibility of compromise at Lambeth, on which the liberals had pinned all their hopes, was killed.

The existence of the Anglican Communion – of Anglican churches outside England grouped into a spiritually and politically significant whole – is theologically mysterious and ontologically doubtful. Historically, however, it is easy to explain. There are Anglican churches everywhere that the British once ruled, and beyond that in countries where Anglican missionaries were active in the nineteenth and early twentieth centuries. By the end of the twentieth century, there were more than forty such churches, which claimed on the basis of extremely dodgy figures to have 80 million members in all. But although they spread under the British crown they were not the result of official policy in the way the Church of England was a part of the English state, except in Ireland and perhaps Wales.

Imperial self-understanding obviously accounted for the existence of the Anglican Communion itself – the constituent churches were almost all in countries that had been British colonies. They had also inherited the internal rivalries of the parties of the Church of England, so that the countries missionized by the evangelical Church Missionary Society grew up with fiercely Protestant churches which abominated homosexuality, while those, like South Africa, where the Society for the Propagation of the Gospel got there first grew Catholic churches, full of ritual, incense and men who felt comfortable in lace. Those two branches still had a certain unity. They agreed on what they disagreed about. Wider and more chaotic disagreements would shake the communion when the Americans started to ordain women. The peculiarly American narrative of successive liberations which had inspired the civil rights movement made much less sense in the rest of the world, though it might seem to have done so briefly in the post-colonial era.

The American Episcopal Church was a curiously mixed body: immensely rich, and with great social cachet, but divided in ways that would soon become familiar across the wider American culture wars. The Southern conservatives were at least to start with bewildered by even the possibility of change. The Northern liberals had an evangelical zeal, a conviction that their democratic and progressive church was a divinely inspired advance on the creaking hierarchical stateliness of the Church of England. Like all the mainstream Protestant denominations, the Episcopalians were losing membership fast in the 1970s and 80s but nothing much could dent their self-confidence. In 1974 the Philadelphia Eleven had been illegally ordained and by 1977 there were women being ordained as priests quite legally in large parts of the USA.

This development faced the Church of England with an existential challenge. It made it impossible to duck the way in which the Church, like the English state, was predicated on the existence of an empire that had actually vanished thirty years before this story opens. From the very beginning, the Anglican Communion had had no central authority. It had never really had a founding moment, though the closest thing would be the Lambeth Conference of 1867, called partly to solve a dispute in the South African church. That summoned all the Anglican bishops of the world to Canterbury, but on the basis that the Conference as such had no authority to bind any of its members. Successive Archbishops of Canterbury had been absolutely clear that no foreign church might tell the Church of England what to do about matters of doctrine or anything else, and had extended this liberty as a matter of courtesy to the other churches. Of course, at the Victorian high noon of empire, they did not need constitutional or legal arrangements to tell other churches what to do, so it cannot have occurred to them that they were giving up any actual or potential power. By the time the possibility was apparent it was far too late.

This was the obvious and outward way in which the imperial experience had shaped the Anglican Communion. There was also a less obvious but ultimately more important sense. This lay in the idea that there should be such a thing as 'Anglicanism' and that this could form a distinctive and important strand of world Christianity. It had its origins in the religious and political convulsions of the Reformation that produced the British imperial state. That ended up defining a 'Church of England' against both Catholic and Protestant dogmatism. The idea of a national church is an odd one. It is not a simple or natural development of Christianity. Jesus' message was a universal one, and so are the aspirations of many of the most vigorous forms of Christianity. The Church of England made sense so long as England was defined by wars against its Catholic or Calvinist neighbours. It was whatever the English believed, and it was given shape much less by doctrine than by the Prayer Book and English culture.

Christians ought to be able to agree without discipline, and for many years it had appeared that the Anglican Communion might offer a model for how they could do so across huge cultural and national boundaries. What, after all, did the church in New Zealand have in common with that in Nigeria, except for the accident that both descended from British colonies? For nearly 150 years, the idea of the Anglican Communion seemed to supply some kind of answer: they cared about each other, and cared to some extent for each other as well. In their most grandiose moments, archbishops even imagined that the Anglican Communion could be a model for the secular world, a sort of UN without tears. Travelling round the world to be feted by enthusiastic Anglicans made a nice change for English bishops and archbishops. Regular trips abroad to meet one another became the mark of aspirational religious leaders, just as it did for legal, political and business elites.

'The great thing about being Archbishop of Canterbury,' said Robert Runcie once, 'is not to believe your own propaganda.' He meant it. Yet even Runcie believed in the Anglican Communion. He spent a huge amount of energy trying to dissuade American bishops from electing a woman as one of their number: a particularly difficult job since it is congregations who choose the bishops in the

USA, and they do not take kindly to being told what to do by their former colonial oppressors.

So Runcie's efforts, though futile, were not hard to understand. The focus of his struggle was the 1988 Lambeth Conference, ten years before the attempted exorcism of Richard Kirker, when the American church, which had already begun to ordain women priests, was threatening to ordain women bishops as well. Women priests were for the bishops like a problem in quantum mechanics: their position and indeed their existence were dependent on the observer. Opponents could and did deny that they were really there at all. But a woman bishop – one of them, who might herself be invited to discuss the problem of her existence – would collapse this hand-waving. Schrödinger's cat would be out of the bag and it would come out very angry.

The issue had split the American church in the 1980s. The argument there was partly on geographic lines, part of the wider American culture wars: liberal Northern coasts pitted against the conservative Southern interior. In a way that would mark the next decades, both sides started to recruit allies and mercenaries from abroad. In 1986, a church in Tulsa, Oklahoma, in the middle of the Bible Belt, flew out the bishop of London, Dr Graham Leonard, to confirm parishioners because it wanted to split from the local bishop who supported the ordination of women, while three years later the church in Massachusetts was contemplating the election of a black, divorced woman bishop.

The liberals represented, were indeed part of, the old anglophile cultural elite in America. They also controlled most of the money, and in effect paid for the Anglican Communion. They certainly paid for the Lambeth Conferences, and the 'Anglican Communion

Office', a tightly knit collection of sinecures which operated with astonishing sloth and inefficiency compared to the conservatives massing on the borders.

The reactionaries had access to streams of un-Anglican funding, notably from the Ahmanson foundations, controlled by a right-wing fundamentalist who wanted to destroy the liberal Protestant denominations of the USA for political reasons. But they lost the battle against women priests quite decisively. It was very clear that they were a minority within the American church: the nature of the religious market in America meant that there were essentially no conservative evangelical Anglicans there, since there were so many other conservative evangelical denominations available, and no advantage comparable to the Church's establishment in England.

In 1988, the best that Runcie could manage was an agreement that the separate churches (known as Provinces) might decide for themselves about women priests. They might, since it was clear that they would.

Less than a year after the 1988 Conference ended, the diocese of Massachusetts consecrated the first woman bishop in the Anglican Communion, a black woman from Washington DC named Barbara Harris. Various conservative groupuscules split off, but the Anglo-Catholic resistance appeared hopeless.

Nine years later, all that had changed. The American conservatives, who had lost over women in the Lambeth Conference of 1988, reappeared in 1998 with massive reinforcements, and this time their chosen cause was homosexuality. They rented the Catholic chaplaincy building on the campus of the University of Kent where the Conference was held, and used it as a base from which to take over the Anglican Communion and destroy the liberal hegemony for ever. One of the things which marked them, then and later, was that they were early and eager in their embrace of what was then known as new technology.

In the basement of the Catholic chaplaincy an enormously fat priest from Dallas – a man so large you could have fitted two of the stouter English traditionalists inside him – presided over five computer screens from which streamed endless messages of encouragement, and anathemas against liberalism. This was the start of the phenomenon of devoted conservatives roaming the ether like lost cats all year round, eager to pounce on godless liberals. A certified public accountant in Tennessee named Deidra Duncan was particularly exercised about the fate of the Church of England. Before the Conference she had sent Andrew an email ('Dear Father Brown') asking for spiritual guidance when she learnt he wrote for the *Church Times*. Andrew explained that he wasn't able to supply the spiritual counsel she desired. Examining her home page on the web, he found a link to a man in Colorado who had proved from the Bible that Prince Charles is the Antichrist. She also rang a vicar in an Essex village, asking for comfort when her cat ran away. Of the five screens in the basement, three carried messages from her.

The conservatives came in endless overlapping groups. The Association for Apostolic Ministry, the Episcopal Synod of America, the American Anglican Council, the Oxford Centre for Mission Studies, Episcopalians United: there were nearly as many varieties of opposition to liberalism as of Trotskyism. But they were all based around Texan money. The English Anglo-Catholics patronized them while they ponced off them. 'Have we shown you the bunker?' they asked, and when questioned about what they were doing in this galère, Stephen Parkinson, the director of Forward in Faith, replied, 'the money, dear boy, the money'.

The Americans would not have been surprised if Bishop Chukwuma had succeeded in his exorcism of Richard Kirker. They believed that homosexuality was a condition that could be cured by the Holy Spirit. But when the American conservatives brought out a couple of men to speak in evangelical terms about their deliverance from homosexuality, the English recoiled fastidiously. Two English Anglo-Catholics took Andrew to supper at an expensive Italian restaurant to avoid the spectacle, but at the end of the evening an English bishop waved him over to where he sat with a tumbler of whisky so he could recite a poem he claimed to have written: 'I thank you Lord, that I am not a fairy: my willy is not brown; my arsehole is still hairy.'

The Americans from the Southern states had organization as well as money and faith. The central Anglican organization, funded by the liberal Northern faction, was unable even to produce a comprehensive list of names and addresses of the bishops attending the Conference. The conservatives produced and published a glossy directory with details and, where possible, photographs of every single bishop. They had prepared for Lambeth by organizing two preliminary conferences in the immediately preceding years for 'two-thirds world' bishops, one in Kuala Lumpur, and one in Dallas. For some of the attendees, this was the first time they had ever been out of Africa. They certainly did not adopt homophobic opinions to please the wealthy Americans and Australians who were bankrolling these meetings: their detestation of homosexuality and liberalism was absolutely sincere. But the conferences allowed for the preparation of agreed statements, or manifestos denouncing homosexuality and other liberal Western vices, which were introduced into all four sections of the Lambeth Conference, not just the one that was meant to be dealing with the topic.

African and Asian churches were not by and large very keen on women priests, but they did not consider them an abomination. Gays were something different. They constituted a much greater affront to godly masculinity. And by 1998, the narrative in the American church had moved on from the liberation of women to the liberation of gay people. This story smashed head on into the growing self-confidence and desire for self-assertion of many of the Asian and African churches. Some of the latter, in particular, saw an opportunity for moral and spiritual leadership. In 1988 it had been a daring and rather contrarian point to observe that there were more churchgoing Anglicans in Nigeria than in England. Ten years later, this would become the basis for a demand that Nigerian values should count for more in the Anglican Communion than English ones.

This truly 'post-colonial' idea – which was of course wholly unacceptable to the vast majority of English churchgoers – seemed plausible to some English bishops for two reasons. The first was the increasing tendency of British evangelicals to seek in the Christianity of the developing world an affirming and enthusiastic credulity about miracles that might counteract the draining scepticism of Europe. In his travels in South America, Bishop David Pytches believed he had seen teeth filled with gold by the Holy Spirit, but such miraculous feats of dentistry proved hard to reproduce in the London suburb of Chorleywood. Another example would be Simon

Barrington-Ward, the bishop of Coventry, who went out to Nigeria as an idealistic curate and felt his tepid, Laodicean faith reproved. He started to believe in the action of evil spirits.

The second was the allure of continuing global significance, after the loss of empire. This was particularly important for Archbishops of Canterbury, who had lost much of their power over the Church in England. The Anglican Communion was a more attractive power base, and the idea that the Archbishop might take his place *ex officio* as a global spiritual leader depended entirely on the existence of the Anglican Communion. It offered bishops and archbishops an importance which was increasingly denied them on the English domestic scene. George Carey would never be greeted in England by cheering crowds of 30,000 or more, but when he went to the Sudan this was routine. It suggested to him that the Sudan might be closer to God. In 1995, George Carey told the General Assembly of the United Nations that 'The Anglican Communion, with 50 million members, has the potential to be a major player on the world stage.'

One never knew with George Carey whether he believed his own propaganda. The figure of 50 million Anglicans was obtained by counting 26 million Anglicans in England, which even Carey must have known was entirely ridiculous. The same year that Carey spoke to the United Nations, Graham Cray, a thoughtful, charismatic evangelical who was then running a theological college in Cambridge, told Andrew the unpalatable truth that 'There is no connection between the belief in God that the majority [in England] tend to have and going to any sort of church. We are a church which gets 3 per cent of the population in its pews and calls itself the national church, in a country where probably three-quarters of the people at large could not tell you what the core doctrines of Christianity are as Christians have expressed them.' This was a problem too large to contemplate. It was probably one reason why evangelicals thought it so important to hold the line on homosexuality: there at least they thought they could be in control, and prevent things changing.

Carey's instinct was to deny that there was any problem with homosexuality among the clergy. Since neither he nor any of his immediate family were gay, he doesn't seem to have regarded the matter as complicated at all. This strategy had already taken a horrible dent in the autumn of 1994, when the General Synod was picketed by members of Outrage! holding up placards naming ten bishops as gay and calling on them to 'Tell The Truth'. Andrew, watching members of the Synod file past the demonstration, was treated to an acidulous commentary from two other spectators, one a married gay priest and the other – also gay – the religious correspondent of the *Daily Telegraph*, a right-wing Roman Catholic. The two men bitched away happily, wondering which bishops had been left off the public list and why. The experience was instructive. It showed Andrew the existence of a widespread and well-established subculture even among the bishops but extending far outside them which official policy could not admit – nor extirpate. Sure enough, three months later the Archbishop of York himself, David Hope, made the announcement that his sexuality was 'a grey area'. Thereafter, it was hard to believe that anything a bishop said on sexuality could be taken at face value, or that the Church of England could ever be purged of its gay clergy.

Although the Outrage! demonstration was immediately denounced as vile and libellous, none of the bishops involved dared sue. The gay lobby had established conclusively that any attempt to drive gay clergy from their posts would be ruinously embarrassing to all concerned.

This was one reason why debate at the Lambeth Conference was so loathsome. The English bishops, at least, knew very well that they were going along with a lie. But they would much rather have done that than have an honest and public disagreement. When the resolution on sexuality was finally debated the carefully planned and fairly balanced resolution which would have kept people talking in committees for years was hijacked from the floor in ways that had been prepared months before in the preliminary conferences in Dallas and Kuala Lumpur. The conservatives put up amendments which stripped all the liberal equivocations away. Even a reference to homophobia was deleted. Instead the Conference condemned 'Unreasonable fear of homosexuals'. This is the hate that dares not speak its name. Carey, on the platform, voted very publicly for every one of the resolutions. 'Those who are supporting [homosexuality],' commented one bishop after the event, 'all of them, we saw their white hands up!' The hot air within the marquee was sharp with masculine sweat and hatred.

The fateful resolution, 'Lambeth 1.10', was supported by 526 bishops, 70 were against, 45 abstained. Carey described it as a 'test case for Anglican unity'. It failed the test.

The gay men present felt they had been the targets of an attempted lynching. One man, the same who had been congratulated by David Hope, then the head of his theological college, when he explained that he had found his life partner in a fellow ordinand, wrote later that 'We are now in a genuinely evil situation, which has arisen directly from a collective decision to collude in a lie. I do not only mean the collusion of the bishops: to some extent we have all succumbed to it … Nevertheless it is disappointing that so few have summoned the moral and intellectual strength to cut through it, or even want to.'

The day after the passing of the sexuality resolution, Andrew went in search of a man who might wash the disgusting taste of self-righteous bullying from his mouth, someone who was even then regarded as unusually holy and unusually clever, even though he was a bishop. Rowan Williams was a scholarship boy from Swansea, who had become a theological wunderkind and a full professor at Oxford by the age of thirty-six.

At Lambeth he was present as the bishop of Monmouth and philosophical heavyweight, who was charged with giving a plenary talk on how to reach moral decisions. It was carefully argued, resonant, thought-provoking, and frequently comprehensible. But for all the effect it had on the assembled bishops, he might have delivered it at three in the morning to the customers in a motorway food court.

He cultivated a slightly shamanic look: sweeping black eyebrows sheltering deep eyes that have green glints in them like the marble you find on the island of Iona, and an intermittently exuberant beard. He seemed a figure entirely alien from the hurrying and striving managers around him. As they stood outside the conference hall, by a choked pond which had once contained small carp, he tried to explain himself: 'Wittgenstein said that the most important thing a philosopher can say to another is "give yourself time". The question is whether we can in some sense bear to keep talking to each other,' he said.

This question would in due course be decisively answered: No.

Much later, though, what seemed to summarize the schism was the way in which Rowan – as everyone always calls him – took for granted (as Andrew did) that Wittgenstein should be an authority to whom Christians should appeal. The future would belong to men who had no time for the opinions of a Jewish gay agnostic.

When Rowan asked Andrew what he made of the Conference, Andrew said that it seemed to be a geological catastrophe. All the ages of Christianity were piled up like beds of rock pushed into mountains. There were Copts from the fifth century, Romans from the fourteenth, Calvinists from the sixteenth, Latitudinarians, Arminians, nineteenth-century fundamentalists, twentieth-century liberals, Pentecostalists, Anglo-Catholics of several generations – and all of these people were calling themselves Anglicans; it was really hard to see why.

He liked this. But, he said, it's important not to think of them all as being the same as they once were. Each style of Christianity has changed or weathered since it first appeared in the rock. Andrew thought this made the analogy more biological: that what we had was a family tree, all descending with different modifications from the original stock of Christianity – and now, of course, we get distinct species and, he rushed on into the analogy, populations that cannot interbreed. Rowan winced, and asked him not to mention breeding. Instead, he talked about an American poet and Benedictine oblate who had written about rediscovering meaning in traditionally religious language; and about the way in which theology could not be understood as a set of propositions. You had to act on it to understand it, he said, and each fresh act of obedience brought new understandings. They were both silent for a moment.

He smiled. 'But still I wonder sometimes why I don't just give up and become an Orthodox.'

It was easy to understand why so many people loved Rowan, and thought him the best hope of the Church of England. Linda first met him when she was an undergraduate at Cambridge in his class on Patristics. It was a surprisingly old-fashioned course. In Rowan's conjuring the Church Fathers floated on and off stage as rather spectral two-dimensional figures, mainly contemplating difficult Christological conundrums, but occasionally dipping reluctantly into the muddy waters of church politics. It was hard not to feel warmth towards this pale, earnest, intellectual fellow creature. Years later, over a lunch with Rowan in Cuddesdon, Linda replied to someone's query about why she became a theologian: 'a lonely childhood'. 'Oh me too,' said Rowan, 'me too.'

Rowan's other-worldliness was bound up with his devout Anglo-Catholicism. This was fertilized with a good dollop of sacramental mysticism derived from deep study of Russian orthodoxy, and seasoned with the chastening, anti-utopian thought of Donald MacKinnon. The younger Rowan was a founding and enthusiastic member of the pro-women's-ordination Affirming Catholicism movement, and was widely viewed as a liberal Catholic. He made a couple of clear statements against what he saw as the sexual atavism of the 1987 Higton resolution, and was a founding trustee of the pro-gay 'Changing Attitude' movement. But in other ways he seemed strikingly conservative. His unique blend of the mystical and the mystifying always made him hard to pin down.

As he advanced up the academic and ecclesiastical ladder, Rowan developed by an apparently organic process into a revered, grey-bearded spiritual teacher. By the time he became Lady Margaret Professor of Divinity and Canon of Christ Church at Oxford, his sermons were attracting crowds of devoted followers. 'What was it about?' Linda once asked a particularly breathless one. 'Oh I don't know,' said the cult worshipper, 'something about the dark being light, and the light being dark. Not sure really, but it was simply marvellous.'

The adulation did not corrupt him too badly. His humility was very deep, if narrow. He always knew he was cleverer than anyone else in the room but he didn't think he was better or closer to God. Years later, Andrew watched him in a room full of murderers in a psychiatric prison (Grendon, in Buckinghamshire) and he was simply wonderful. He sat on a plain chair in a chapel which had windows whose panes were separated not by lead but by thick concrete, in circles rather smaller than a man could squeeze through. The men who entered were not quite usual either. A couple wore rosaries or crosses. Two or three looked hard, with tattoos and sharp muscles, but most just seemed middle-aged and rather tired. They sat in a loose circle in front of the Archbishop. He did not preach or pray. They began to introduce themselves, exactly as they would if he were a new inmate.

'I'm doing life for murder, coming off a drug episode ... I've been thirty-four years inside. Doing life for murder, been here before. I have difficulties dealing with people in authority ... I'm doing life for killing my girlfriend ... Indecent assault ... murder ... armed robbery, shooting, kidnap. I want to be a husband, and a father to my kids ... A life sentence for killing my wife ... I spent fifteen of the last seventeen years in prison for robbery. I come here to deal with my emotions. It's a very hard place when you can't run away from your emotions … murder of a drug dealer.'

When they had introduced themselves they asked Rowan questions. He talked about his daily prayer in the most careful, practical way, almost as if it were therapy: 'Breathe regularly, sit upright, breathe, and say some simple words. I will often say "Lord have mercy" slowly, at intervals, and just let it settle into my stomach. It doesn't always seem to work. Sometimes I can be there for half an hour and the thoughts just go galloping round like horses in the Grand National. Then I have to remind myself that this is time God gives to me, and not just time I give to God.' Then, in the same matter-of-fact way, he said: 'You are trying to open the cellar door and be aware of the darkness underneath the water.'

It was the closest he came to formal preaching, or even to talking about Jesus. When he prayed at the end of a meeting, he did not once mention sin or forgiveness but talked, without affectation, as if healing and honesty were things that all of us needed. It's not a bad epitaph on a Christian that he should have been more at home with murderers than with ecclesiastical politicians. Unfortunately, an archbishop must spend less time with murderers than with other prelates.

It's easy, looking back on the 1998 Lambeth Conference, to suppose that what was most terrible about it was that the wrong side won. The only thing that anyone will remember was 'Lambeth 1.10', the resolution on sexuality, which gave a quasi-legal backing to subsequent attempts to drive gay people from the Church. But what was actually more shocking was the vanity, the naked politicking between clerical camps, and the absence of any suggestion of the things that might make going to church worthwhile. In this the liberals were almost as guilty as the conservatives. Shortly before Lambeth had begun, Jack Spong, the Episcopalian Bishop of Newark, had referred to African Christians as 'superstitious' and 'yet to face the intellectual revolution of Copernicus and Einstein'. He later apologised for using the word 'superstitious'. In 1998 it was still possible for some Americans to believe that history had ended and all that remained was a mopping-up operation: the more backward parts of the world would adopt the moral codes of American suburbia as naturally as they had taken up its fast-food chains.

A smog compounded of clerical self-importance and – increasingly – self-pity hung over Lambeth as it would hang over the remaining years of the Anglican Communion and its interminable, terminal arguments about homosexuality. Andrew, who had for years seen himself on the fringes of Christianity, drove away from it for the last time resolved never to be mistaken for a Christian again.

# 9

# The Rowan vacuum

Somewhere on that drive home from the Lambeth Conference Andrew stopped at a motorway service station and realized that it was the first time in three weeks that he had heard Estuary English. None of the bishops on the campus at Canterbury talked like the English people who surrounded their churches. Even George Carey, who had grown up in Dagenham, had acquired unique but somewhat plummy tones during his ascent through the Church. He could no more speak the language 'understanded of the common people' than could any of the other bishops.

A lovely illustration of this came in 1997, when he broadcast his Christmas message from a service held on a Sunday afternoon in an Asda supermarket to all the other ones in the country. The hapless shoppers were handed service sheets and expected to sing along as they manoeuvred their trolleys. This was not a plan which would have occurred to anyone who knew people who had never gone to church, or even anyone who had ever done any shopping on the Sunday before Christmas.

It was just a tiny symptom of the general and growing detachment of the Church from the England around it. There were larger ones.

The death and funeral rites of Diana were a gigantic upswelling of post-Christian sentiment. Someone described the milling crowd which formed in front of Kensington Palace after the news of her death as 'a congregation without a church'. The rituals that emerged – the teddy bears, the flowers, the huge crowds – were not orchestrated by religion. George Carey went round the country for months afterwards giving speeches in which he claimed that this showed a deep spiritual hunger in the nation, which the Church stood ready to feed. But no one wanted what the Church was offering and no one in the Church seemed to give serious thought to the dimensions of the problem.

A similar failure attended the absurd Millennium Dome, which seems to have been intended as a post-Christian, or a-Christian, celebration of British spirituality – except that the word 'spirituality' was confined to a 'spirit zone', which had no taint of holiness or danger. Carey lobbied furiously for a year to get the Church officially represented at the opening, which in the event turned into a monumental fiasco. Guests were delayed for hours in East London, the acts were ghastly, and at the end of the evening, the Queen turned to one of her companions and said, 'Well, there were only two people who enjoyed that – George Carey and Cherie Blair.'

The interest surrounding his successor was considerable. Among the chattering classes, and all across the media, there was a feeling – despite Diana, despite the Millennium Dome – that Christianity might be much more interesting than Carey had made it seem.

Carey's own choice for his successor seems to have been Michael Nazir-Ali, the bishop of Rochester. Nazir-Ali, the child of Pakistani converts, had been at one stage the youngest Anglican bishop in the world. His diocese in Pakistan had been the subject of persecution by Muslims. He understood viscerally that Christianity is now a global religion and that the Church of England does not matter much within that frame. That much he had in common with Rowan Williams, but the Christianity he preferred to societal Anglicanism was a hard-edged Protestantism instead of Rowan's mysticism. He was clever and interested in ideas, but his candidacy withered under public scrutiny.

If Nazir-Ali was the candidate of the right, and Rowan that of the left, the conservative candidate was Richard Chartres, the bishop of London, who had once been Robert Runcie's chaplain. Tall, socially assured and with great theatrical presence, he was far too clever to be an intellectual. He was also the only candidate then or later to run a diocese that was seriously worried about the ageing and numerical decline of its congregations, and made real efforts to deal with it. This was partly because the diocese of London was home to HTB, with which Chartres was careful to maintain friendly relations, and partly because the city of London is full of religious fervour by comparison with the surrounding country – largely because of migration and good Church of England schools with places reserved for churchgoers. But geography alone could not explain the relative success of the diocese of London, since it only covers the city north of the Thames. The southern half is known to the Church of England as the diocese of Southwark, and despite a similar population has shown a pattern of unremitting fissiparous decline for decades.

Chartres' particular political skill lay in suggesting that he held very strong positions without ever entirely committing himself to any of them. His opposition to women priests ruled him out of the running, yet he was the only really credible candidate apart from Rowan Williams.

By now, though, women priests were not the issue that they had once been. Just as had earlier happened in the USA and at the Lambeth conferences, the arguments had hardened and the trenches had been dug on the question of homosexuality. Williams was both the leading theological defender of gay Christians and one of their most practical protectors. As a young man he had seriously considered leaving the Church of England over the persecution of gay clergy. As bishop of Monmouth he had a gay priest, Martin Reynolds, living with his partner, as his neighbour and friend; the two men were, with Williams's knowledge, fostering a severely disturbed adolescent boy.

Such a man, it seemed obvious to everyone, would end the discrimination of the Carey years. What was more, he might be able to talk about Christianity in ways that brought it alive to people who would not think of entering a church from one year's end to the next. He had a knack for talking as if he understood doubt without sharing it. He told a Christian magazine that when praying 'Just for a second you think "this actually might be real", and then it's back to normal and a lot of brick walls, a sense of treading water and the only thing that gives you any sense that it's real is that you are still doing it somehow.'

In one of his published sermons he described the Book of Revelation as 'tightly written, pen driving into the cheap paper, page after page of paranoid fantasy and malice, like the letters clergymen so frequently get from the wretched and disturbed'.

By 2002 he was in receipt of an unusual number of such letters. Some contained actual dog shit. The campaign to succeed Carey, undeclared though it was, was conducted with astonishing displays of spite and venom on both sides. Michael Nazir-Ali was denounced anonymously to some newspapers: he was supposed to have lied about his age and to have faked some of his academic qualifications. Both these accusations were entirely false. So was the rumour fed to one religious correspondent that Rowan Williams, while at Oxford, had attended gay orgies organized by his best man, Christopher Morgan – who was at the time of the rumours the religious correspondent of the *Sunday Times*.

Some of the charges against Williams were actually justified. He did support gay clergy and had provided one of the most powerful theological justifications for their love and sex lives in his published lecture 'The Body's Grace'. When press reports claimed that Reynolds and his partner were considering adoption, Martin Reynolds – the evening before the story appeared – handed in his permission to officiate, in order save Williams embarrassment. Williams could not at first see why this was necessary. For a long time he could not understand how very much he was despised by his evangelical opponents.

When he, who took his Welshness seriously, was honoured as a Druid at an Eisteddfod, *The Times* put the ceremony on its front page under the headline '"Hairy leftie" Archbishop joins the druids'. He invited the Church Society, representing the most uncharismatic puritans, to lunch: their representatives appeared and claimed to have already eaten. They watched him eat his sandwiches unaccompanied. They would not share a meal with a heretic.

What they failed to notice is that he was already moving towards the conclusion that it was his duty, as Archbishop, to abandon his unpopular principles.

From the moment his election was confirmed, he had spoken as if he had assumed a duty to equivocate to the point of frank dishonesty about his views on sexuality. In his farewell address to the diocese of Monmouth, he assured them that he had 'always been committed to the church's traditional teaching on sex before marriage', a remark which even his most admiring biographer, Rupert Shortt, found impossible to swallow. When he appeared on *Desert Island Discs*, he assured the presenter that he had never gone against the advice he had received when ordaining men who might be gay. This, says Shortt, would not have been seen by his former colleagues as 'an accurate description of the broader picture'. Honesty apart, it was a curious policy for him to adopt. It could not appease his enemies, who would not be satisfied with anything less than grovelling repentance, and it would have scandalized his friends had they noticed it. None did. The one thing everyone knew about Rowan was that he was a principled defender of gay people.

The conservative evangelicals – among them George Carey's son Andrew, who worked as a journalist– had fought him tooth and nail, down to the last minute. A week before his enthronement they held a conference at Stott's old church to announce that sexuality was 'a first-order issue', meaning that those who took the liberal line on sexuality were not in fact real Christians. It was not enough for Rowan as Archbishop to do what they wanted, or to refrain from what they did not want him to do. 'We want repentance. We want him to repent,' said a Reform spokesman.

The opposition to him only strengthened the belief that his supporters had in him. He was clearly a scholar, possibly a saint, and certainly very interesting, a man whose courage and capacity for plain speaking about subtle matters would rejuvenate the Church of England. With Rowan at the helm there would no longer be any need for that slight cringe which any educated Christian felt when George Carey stepped up to proclaim the faith with his trademark lack of doubt or credibility. When his election as Archbishop was confirmed in December 2002, it looked as if the Church of England would be led by a public intellectual of the first rank, for the first time since William Temple had helped lay the foundations of the welfare state in the 1940s.

It took him six months to wreck the illusion.

The post of bishop of Reading is one of the quintessential middle-management jobs of the Church of England. The bishop is one of the three assistants in the diocese of Oxford. He (or today, possibly she) looks after the prosperous corridor along the M4 west of London; around 800,000 people live in this area, which means that there may be as many as 20,000 in church on any given Sunday. The town of Reading had been a citadel of old-fashioned gin and lace Anglo-Catholicism, with its characteristic blend of high seriousness and high camp: it was the headquarters of Brian Brindley in his days of pomp, before the *News of the World* turned him over, but it also had a conservative evangelical presence. The diocese of Oxford itself was the home base of many of the conservative groups which had organized the coup at the Lambeth Conference in 1988. The bishop, Richard Harries, was a 'don't ask, don't tell' liberal in the Runcie mode who had done his best to protect Brian Brindley.

The previous bishop of Reading, Dominic Walker, was an Anglo-Catholic bachelor whose only public eccentricity was an interest in exorcism. He replaced Rowan in Monmouth and eventually retired to Brighton. Jeffrey John, though also Anglo-Catholic, was a very different character. We've met him before as a young ordinand who was encouraged in his relationship by the head of his theological college. He had been openly gay throughout his career in the Church, and had written a pamphlet, *Permanent, Stable, Faithful*, upholding some gay relationships as a Christian pattern. He was also, like his friend Rowan, a man with a very high doctrine of the Church. He had stayed with the same partner, Grant Holmes, since they had met at theological college, but their relationship had been celibate since the mid-1990s. John was a gifted preacher and as a canon of Southwark Cathedral was widely admired. Had it not been for his unrepentant, if hardly flaunted, gay identity he would have been a bishop long before.

So he was not even considered in the first rounds of selection for the post, after Dominic Walker had gone to Monmouth. Only after the Archbishops' appointments secretary, Tony Sadler, had sent to Oxford a list of four names with John's starred as the outstanding candidate, did the diocese begin to consider him. Then he became the outstanding candidate, based both on his CV and on his performance at an interview panel. After the event, Rowan's supporters did their best to blame Richard Harries for the fiasco but this was neither dignified nor truthful. At the time, Harries was not a campaigner for gay rights, and he told his diocesan synod that 'I was very reluctant to include Jeffrey John on the list of candidates at first. His homosexuality was a major factor to consider ... I looked very carefully at the references to his lifestyle.' But after interviewing him, Harries was convinced that he was the outstanding candidate. His lifestyle was within the boundaries set by the Church, and he had won over the evangelical clergy in the diocese of Southwark. Harries believed that within a couple of years he would do the same in Oxford.

The pressure against John was slow to mount. It could not have happened without the internet: as so often happens, a movement which is profoundly reactionary in social terms was years ahead of the times when it came to the adoption of technology. Without the internet no one in England would have known or cared what was said in Nigeria. Without the internet, no one in Nigeria would have read Jeffrey John's remarkably honest and thoughtful account of his life as a gay man in the Church, originally delivered as a speech to the Anglo-Catholics of Southwark. It had been preserved on a website, then taken down, then excavated by evangelical campaigners.

Rowan Williams is not of course gay. But his theological position on the matter and Jeffrey John's were more or less identical. Both men believed in permanent, faithful and stable relationships. Both men believed that it was sometimes the right thing for gay people to have gay sex. Both men supposed that it was the duty of a priest and still more of a bishop to follow the direction of the Church but the duty of a theologian sometimes to argue against it.

So any attack on Jeffrey John on the grounds that his views disqualified him to hold an insignificant job in the Church of England was *a fortiori* an attack on Rowan Williams that would disqualify him from holding a much more important and significant job, since the conservatives claimed, and some may even have believed, that their objections were entirely to John's beliefs and not to his actions.

This made the assault on Jeffrey John's appointment irresistible to people who believed that Rowan Williams should not be Archbishop of Canterbury, and who had spent the preceding year or so trying to stop him. Richard Harries, at least, was well aware of this aspect. He spoke twice to Rowan to be assured of his continued backing for Jeffrey John. Each time he was reassured. The opposition mounted steadily. Nine English bishops publicly denounced the proposed appointment. Eight others released a letter cheering it on. Archbishop Akinola of Nigeria, who saw himself as the true leader of the Anglican Communion, announced that Jeffrey John must not have the job. So did Archbishop Drexel Gomez of the West Indies. Evangelicals announced that as many as a hundred parishes might refuse to pay into diocesan funds if the appointment went ahead.

This was the tactic first suggested in 1987 by David Holloway of Jesmond, in Newcastle, who co-wrote the Higton resolution. In the intervening years it had grown more popular, until it was unofficially practised by almost all the churches that could credibly threaten to do it. Had anyone sat down to do the arithmetic (as some years later was actually done) they would have discovered that the threat to do more was largely empty because all of the big conservative evangelical churches had already gone into internal and undeclared schism.

How much any parishioners cared is very much harder to know. Harries had not wanted this fight, but now it had been taken on he understood the importance of victory. Jeffrey John had been properly chosen by the correct procedures and had promised to uphold the teaching of the Church of England in word and deed quite as much as Rowan did. To back down would be to hand the conservative evangelicals – represented by two large and rich churches in his diocese – a veto over all diocesan appointments and to formalize what had been the informal view under George Carey that no one of ostentatiously liberal views – what Carey would call in his own scare quotes 'unbelieving bishops' – should ever be promoted into the public eye.

Harries' presidential address to his diocesan synod, calling for a 'gay friendly Oxford diocese', was warmly received in the hall. Over the next few weeks private meetings were arranged between the prospective bishop and prominent Berkshire evangelical clergy. Not all were won over, but many were personally very impressed by him. A meeting of Berkshire Area Deans and Lay Chairs held shortly before his candidacy was withdrawn found sixteen out of twenty to be supportive, with two implacably opposed, and two deanery lay chairs understanding but uncertain how to sell the idea of a gay bishop of Reading to their deaneries.

It seemed clear that all Rowan needed to do was to hold his nerve and the fuss would be wholly forgotten in six months.

But Rowan could not hold his nerve. On Friday July 4th he summoned Jeffrey John and Richard Harries to a meeting at Lambeth the next morning (John was to wear civilian clothes lest anyone spot him) and when they arrived he told them that John must withdraw his candidacy. This had to be done by John himself, since there was no other way by which Rowan could be extricated from the difficulty of appointing him now that all the formal hazards had been cleared. Neither man had had any inkling that this was coming.

After several hours, Jeffrey John finally submitted to his old friend's request, but refused to sign the form of words prepared by Lambeth which implied that he was withdrawing of his own volition. The next morning, before the surrender could be announced, George Carey revealed on the *Sunday* programme that he had ordained two celibate gay bishops himself. John, increasingly outraged, rang Lambeth Palace to withdraw his resignation. The offer was ignored and although there are claims that it never reached Rowan and the whole debacle was the fault of his staff, these are very hard to credit. Jeffrey John's withdrawal of his candidacy was publicly announced as if he'd never rung the Palace and everyone knew that Rowan had forced him to do it.

In one morning's work he had betrayed his friend, his principles and those subordinates who'd put their trust in him. The nearest he ever came to a public explanation was his reported remark to the House of Bishops that the reasons for which he eventually said 'no' were the same reasons as had led him in the first place to say 'yes': he thought he had always acted for the well-being of the church. For Richard Harries it was a 'Damascus Road experience' after which he became actively pro-gay on all legislative matters. For Rowan the impact was rather different. Although he was to remain in office for another ten years, he was never after that in power. Of course, by the standards of normal politics, this was a very minor treachery, a perfectly prudent cowardice. But judged by the standards of normal politics it was also extraordinarily stupid; even if not a terrible crime it was certainly a dreadful mistake. He never had, then or later, an answer to the question that Alan Rusbridger of the *Guardian* asked him in an interview once: 'Why should anyone care what you think when we know that you won't stand up for it?' beyond the rueful charming thing he actually said, which was 'Ouch!'

Rowan himself gained nothing by his betrayal of Jeffrey John. Perhaps that is how he justified his action to himself but on any reasonable scheme of morality that just makes his action worse. God – presumably God – wanted him to be Archbishop of Canterbury and to take the decisions that an archbishop must. To hand over that power to his enemies was to reject the giver as well as the gift.

The years immediately afterwards were bad ones. One of his bishops remarked long afterwards, 'I think he fell into a depression because he could not reconcile what he had done with the person he thought he was. When I am a shit to someone, that's just a bad day at the office; but this was Rowan, saint and scholar. He couldn't be a shit – and yet he had been one.'

Nor were his enemies satisfied with their victory. The logic of Rowan's position was one of mutual concession: if he gave them what they wanted, they should respond with forbearance towards the difficulties of others, and all the bishops together should worry at the truth like patient followers of Wittgenstein. But the Anglican Communion was not a philosophy seminar but a game played on playground rules. The weak were there to be bullied and the quiet to be shouted down. Rowan had seen all this – or at least he'd witnessed it – at Lambeth five years before. Now it would be demonstrated again and again.

The first problem arose in the USA. The liberal majority of bishops and clergy in the American church had never felt bound by the resolutions of the Lambeth Conference; in any case, they were directly elected by the people of their dioceses. The complex institutional loyalties of the Church of England, and its commitment to balance, could not develop or thrive under such a system. In a societal church all kinds of people and theologies must learn to rub along together and they will in time make a virtue of this affliction. This process wasn't perfect even in England, as we have seen in the complete mutual incomprehension and separate lives of two such priests as Tony Higton and Jeffrey John, neither of whom could suppose the other was properly Anglican. But at least it was held up as an ideal. It was part of the self-understanding of the Church of England. It would not have been part of the self-understanding of the Anglican Communion had that been coherent enough to have a self-understanding. And in the free religious market of the USA that kind of toleration made no sense at all. There, if you found yourself sharing a church with people who were both wrong and repulsive you just got up and left. So when the electors of the diocese of New Hampshire came to choose a new bishop in the summer of 2003 – five years to the day after resolution 1.10 was carried at Lambeth – the fact that one of the candidates was gay and living with his partner did not bother many of them at all.

They certainly could not care in the slightest what Nigerian Christians thought of their choice, nor archbishops in England, nor, really, the hierarchy of the Episcopal Church in the USA. They liked Gene Robinson. They knew him, for he had worked among them for eleven years. And in August 2003 they elected him.

The immediate consequence was that he was advised by the police to wear a bulletproof vest on his public appearances. This advice still held when he visited Britain the following year.

The election, and its ratification by the national church that summer, four weeks after Rowan had forced Jeffrey John to resign, led to the split in the American church which both sides had been working for at least since Lambeth. This was not quite what either side had wanted. Both had hoped it would remain whole, but expel their opponents. It is possible that some of the money which kept the Southern conservatives going was paid by right-wing political interests which did want the Episcopal Church to split, to become weak and fragmented – a similar assault was mounted on the liberal Methodist denomination in the USA – but the property, the pensions and the prestige of an undivided church were all attractive to the people inside it. Once the conservatives had realized, in the autumn after Gene Robinson's consecration, that the liberals had managed to bring all the church's property under central, and so liberal, control in the course of the ructions about ordaining women, they shifted their efforts to the international arena. Since they could not be validated by their own bishops, they would find others. If they could not force the liberals out of the Episcopal Church, they should force the Episcopal Church out of the Anglican Communion.

The demeaning and ultimately futile attempts to halt a schism are outside the scope of this book, except in as much as they had effects on the ground in England. They took up a great deal of Rowan's time. You might liken his belief in churches to his belief in people. Just as he supposed that people are constituted and brought into being by their relationships with other people and ultimately with God, he treated the Anglican Communion as something which would come into a meaningful existence if only other, similar bodies would treat it as if it were one. Indeed, he seems to have

thought that the Church of England could only be a real church
if the Church of Nigeria (for example) thought it was one. This
identification of political and theological reality is difficult for most
people to maintain if they are to remain Christians. The problem
of petty evil is much more troubling to the honest believer than
the problem of great evil – partly because it's much more obvious
and so much harder to struggle against. It is in some ways easier to
believe that great evil in the abstract is necessary for God's purposes
than that the petty stupidities and self-importance of a bureaucracy
and the foetid hatreds of a Lambeth Conference are a testament to
His existence.

In any case, the effort that Rowan Williams spent on diplomacy
was almost entirely wasted. The conclusion that everyone drew from
the Jeffrey John affair was that he could be bullied and so he was.
But he was trapped. He could not arrange for the victory of his own
ideas, whatever those by now might be, but neither could he deliver
the surrender of the people who had once been his followers. The
liberals were defeated, demoralized and confused, but they would
not abandon their convictions.

Had the schism in the Anglican Communion actually been
a disagreement between national churches, it is possible that the
Archbishop could have delivered a workable compromise. But in
fact he was caught up in the fight between two American factions,
both of which could settle for nothing less than the extirpation
of the other, and alongside that a struggle with African churches
which saw in the American factionalism an opportunity to expand
their own influence. Ecclesiologically, they were reversing the old
patterns of colonialism, where the European powers had gained

their empires by exploiting divisions among the natives. Now the Nigerian and Rwandan churches set up subsidiaries in the USA and demanded that these be recognized as the true Anglicans there. In England, too, the Rwandans formed links with one of the oldest and most successful of the HTB church plants – St Mark's, Battersea Rise. Sandy Millar, who had transformed HTB, retired and was promptly consecrated as a missionary bishop, in England, for the Ugandan Anglican Church, one of the most sincerely homophobic bodies in the Anglican Communion.

Many of the Africans and a few Asians split off into a body called GAFCON, which maintained it was still Anglican, and started to issue declarations and statements of faith to which all other provinces must sign up if they were to be considered Anglican too. Michael Nazir-Ali joined them, and along with over 250 other bishops boycotted the 2008 Lambeth Conference.

But he was the only English diocesan bishop to do so. Efforts to 'realign' the more fervent conservative evangelical parishes of the Church of England so that they were tightly allied with the Church of Nigeria came up against the same problem as efforts towards unity with the Roman Catholics had done: a small number of clergy cared passionately but very few laypeople cared at all and those who did were perfectly free to move rather than wait for the organization to shift. If you prefer African Christianity to English, there are hundreds, possibly thousands of congregations in London alone which you can join. Only if your pension is paid by the Church of England does it seem terribly important that there be a corporate realignment.

Rowan and his staff tried to put sex behind them (so to speak). He had so much to say about so many other things. His opposition to the Iraq War was well known and prescient. But it was expressed with enough reservations to get him condemned both for what he meant and for his failure to say it. Besides, there was a deeper problem which does not seem to have been understood by his staff. Neither he nor anyone who worked for him seem to have understood that his opinions on Iraq were no more interesting than Rusbridger's views on the Church. In both cases, they were views from the sidelines.

The reason journalists asked him about gay clergy was that this was a decision he could actually make. In that argument he was not just an interested spectator. This was a distinction which seemed to him and, at first, to many of his supporters, quite irrelevant. Surely what mattered was the illumination he could bring to any subject on which he brought his intellect and holiness to bear.

The idea that the nation should be grateful for his thought led to the second defining catastrophe of his period in office. In 2007 he read a book that interested him on the role of parallel legal systems in Israel. He determined to give a speech or a lecture about the issues that it raised. A talk to the Inner Temple offered an opportunity, and Lambeth Palace approached Christopher Landau, a former pupil of Rowan's who was then the BBC's religious correspondent, to see if he could make a story of it.

Landau was an excellent journalist, quick, accurate, scrupulous and well informed. Later he would give up the business to get himself ordained. If anyone could make an academic lecture on the overlapping social identities presupposed by the legal systems of multi-faith societies interesting it was Landau. As he later told the story, he was in despair for a news line as Rowan worked his way through his thoughts about how the law had to take into account religious beliefs.

The lecture he was supposed to turn into a news story was constructed from sentences like this one (yes, just one):

> The rule of law is thus not the enshrining of priority for the universal/abstract dimension of social existence but the establishing of a space accessible to everyone in which it is possible to affirm and defend a commitment to human dignity as such, independent of membership in any specific human community or tradition, so that when specific communities or traditions are in danger of claiming finality for their own boundaries of practice and understanding, they are reminded that they have to come to terms with the actuality of human diversity – and that the only way of doing this is to acknowledge the category of 'human dignity as such' – a non-negotiable assumption that each agent (with his or her historical and social affiliations) could be expected to have a voice in the shaping of some common project for the well-being and order of a human group.

This didn't impress all the lawyers present. One said afterwards that 'Rowan's view on law is unique and so theoretical as to be virtually meaningless. It coincides neither with the Roman law concepts of civic governance nor with natural or divine law theory.'

Neither did it offer much to an ignorant audience. So Landau decided to find something usable through an interview, and after about twenty minutes of waffling asked Rowan whether he thought that the adoption of Sharia really was necessary for community cohesion. To this Rowan replied, 'It seems unavoidable and indeed as a matter of fact certain provisions of Sharia are already recognised in our society and under our law. So it's not as if we're bringing in an alien and rival system.'

There's a sense in which the ensuing debacle was dreadfully unfair. It was a throwaway remark which no reasonably well-informed observer could deny. Of course it was true that Sharia law was unavoidable, in the sense that there were, and still are, Sharia tribunals already operating in England, and there is no obvious legal way to shut them down. If private citizens wish to seek their assistance and abide by the results, there is nothing that can stop them. The law can say that certain penalties are unenforceable, or possibly illegal. It can no more ban the courts themselves than it can ban the laws of football.

But to say that it was not like the introduction of an alien and rival system really was remarkably obtuse. Sharia appeared to most non-Muslims as the quintessence of an alien and rival system; it's probably fair to say that it appeared that way to its enthusiasts as well. Rowan was dimly aware of this. He went on to say that 'Sharia does have this very clear image in people's minds, whether it's stoning or what might happen to a woman who's been raped. These are big hurdles to overcome if you're trying to rehabilitate Sharia.' But instead of addressing this very clear image, he continued to talk as if he were giving Landau a tutorial. He was much more interested in his own ideas than those of his audience on the radio.

He'd done the reading. He'd done the thinking. He just hadn't done the bit where you check your conclusions with someone who knows what you're talking about. And in his excitement at discovering a whole new world of subtle differentiations he managed to strike a nerve in the much wider population, which couldn't care about the Church, but did care about England. By saying that Sharia was 'unavoidable', he played perfectly into the deepest fears about the decline or disappearance of England, which the decline of his own church appeared to be modelling.

Only a month before, Michael Nazir-Ali had been in the headlines for claiming that Muslims had set up 'no go' areas in England already, though he declined to name and identify any. Now there was an Archbishop of Canterbury who seemed to say this was quite all right and there was nothing particularly Christian about being English. But if there was no link between Englishness and Christianity, what was the point of the Church of England?

Perhaps Rowan could have rescued himself, or his staff could have rescued him, by a vigorous campaign of explanation. But vigour was by then beyond them. In the event, Lambeth Palace said nothing for six hours after the interview went out at lunchtime, while the soundbite spread across the world. The press office claimed that if people really wanted to know what the Archbishop thought they should read his whole speech. But no one was interested in what the Archbishop really thought. The public excitement was all about something he hadn't thought, and didn't mean to say.

By the time this had sunk in, it was too late. The Sharia debacle did for his reputation among people who don't care at all about church politics pretty much what the Jeffrey John affair had already done for those who did, and even more than the Jeffrey John affair it was entirely self-inflicted.

# 10

# Where England went

One obvious question is why no one helped Rowan, or indeed the Church of England, avoid the ditches into which they repeatedly fell. After all, this was the established religion of the country, and one might have imagined that someone would start to worry.

The answer in relation to Rowan personally is that a lot of his friends did try to help. Many reported that they offered support, but received no response. 'I think Rowan basically made decisions alone, by going into Lambeth Palace chapel for two hours and emerging and making the decision,' said a senior bishop from that time. 'You can talk again and again and again to people whom you might judge to have been his friends, and find they have never been sounded out or consulted on anything.' Perhaps Rowan thought he had no need of advice. Perhaps the offers never got through. Rowan surrounded himself with a protective staff which behaved as if he were a rare animal that must be treated with great care to survive in captivity.

When it came to the ever more hopeless decline of the Church of England during Rowan's time in Lambeth, however, the explanation for non-intervention is more complicated.

The body with most responsibility was Parliament. Leaving aside the role of the monarch, it was ultimately Parliamentarians, acting on behalf of the people of England, who had oversight of the Church. But Parliament had ceased to care. The few MPs who used to, like Frank Field on the left, or John Gummer on the right, had either converted to Catholicism, or come close to retirement. The official bridge between the government of the day and the Church, the Second Estates Commissioner, did his best, but the point in proceedings when the House of Commons discussed Church questions had become the point at which MPs left to do something more important.

As for the House of Lords, the fact that twenty-six Church of England bishops sat there by right seemed to make things worse, not better. For one thing, few were there very often. In any case, the bishops' presence had a deadening effect on debates about church-related matters. Discussions about what to do concerning 'redundant' church buildings, for example, are full of platitudinous speeches about what a wonderful part of our heritage they are, and how someone needs to take care of them. Courtesy seems to inhibit members of the House of Lords from asking hard questions of the 'Lords Spiritual' about what is going wrong in their own back garden.

The existence of the General Synod was an additional factor in this general failure of critical input, because it gave the illusion of some form of lay involvement and democratic governance, while serving to render it almost completely useless. Something similar can be said about most PCCs. The power that laypeople used to exercise within the Church by way of patronage, Parliament and voluntary societies had been whittled away in the course of the twentieth century, as the Church became increasingly clerical. Even the smallest lay role at local level – like preaching – required an onerous process of diocesan-approved training and certification.

The Church Commissioners didn't help. Their financial success, minus one major jolt, combined with the extraordinary generosity of ageing congregations in making up the shortfall, masked the problem of decline. They allowed the Church to keep trading, but prevented it from receiving the signals that would reach any normal organization when people stop using its services.

And the media lost interest. Journalists like Ruth Gledhill used to keep a watchful eye out for any kind of hypocrisy or scandal, and make the most of it when they spotted it. But religious correspondents were cut as newspapers tried to save money, and the Church of England was freed from yet another check on its behaviour. What's more, it had exempted itself from the rules which kept other public bodies on the straight and narrow, rules about non-discrimination, and rules about transparency. Unlike politicians, who are voted out of office if people don't like what they do, senior clergy are utterly and wholly unaccountable to those they serve.

The upshot was that the balance between church, state and society which is the only real justification for religious establishment fell into ever greater disequilibrium, with each element spinning off into its own orbit.

By the time Rowan took office, academics had spent a long time trying to understand church decline in Britain. Between the years 2000 and 2002 Linda had been immersed in the town of Kendal in Cumbria with a team of colleagues, looking at the situation at ground level. The Kendal research, presented in the book *The Spiritual Revolution*, discovered not just the unremarkable fact that the churches were declining, but the more surprising one that alternative forms of spirituality disconnected from the churches were growing. Fast.

In the small town of Kendal there were 126 groups and providers who described what they did as spiritual, alongside 25 Christian congregations. The spiritual activities ranged from yoga groups, to Reiki healing, to an interfaith group, and varied kinds of meditation practice. Their prime movers were nearly all women, and a large proportion were refugees from the NHS, the Church of England, or both. A generation before, or in different circumstances, they would have been giving their energies to the Church.

Towards the end of this research, Linda met Rowan at Lambeth Palace, and began to tell him what the Kendal Project had found. The conversation stalled. The temperature dropped. It really was as if a shutter came down. He just didn't want to know.

This experience would be repeated with audiences across the country. In a seminar at Durham University, the retired bishop of Ely, Stephen Sykes, became indignant about the use of the word 'spirituality' in relation to Kendal, remonstrating that it was a Christian concept which belonged to the church. When it was gently pointed out that this was how people were using the word, he retorted that they had no business doing so.

Burgeoning popular forms of spirituality were regularly dismissed in sermons and theology as flaky at best, narcissistic at worst. But this wasn't what the team found in Kendal, where most of the practitioners impressed as sincere and responsible. Their implicit theology was that divine Spirit was at work wherever there was healing, wholeness and honesty – and this wasn't so different from what liberal Anglicans used to think too. Those who sought them out came from across the social classes, with problems which ranged from a bad back to terminal cancer, or from serious depression to a vague sense of life unfulfilled. In many cases, they reported that they'd been helped. Some went on to set up stall themselves.

This luxuriant undergrowth of spirituality in Britain, of which Kendal gave just a glimpse, proved more threatening to the Church than angry atheism, other faiths, or bland indifference – all of which had also been on the rise since the late 1980s. Rowan enjoyed debating with Richard Dawkins, and made alliances with other conventional faith leaders. Interfaith work was deemed a good thing. But the fact that ordinary people, particularly women, were doing spiritual things for themselves and others, completely independent of 'religious professionals', was unpalatable, and the idea that they might even have something to teach the Church was totally unthinkable.

Ironically, Rowan was the very person who might have been able to reconnect such spirituality with the English church and its mystical traditions: with Julian of Norwich, William Blake, Thomas Traherne, Evelyn Underhill. This was the time when Susan Howatch was selling stacks of novels about historic Anglicans with a spiritual bent. Rowan himself had a deep and attractive personal spirituality, and his writings developed a profound mystical theology. But he preferred the mysticism of Russian Orthodoxy to that of England.

At the heart of Rowan's spiritual writings was the idea that, since God was greater than anything we can imagine or speak of, as soon as we refer to God we need to qualify what we say. God is not some super-person, some father-figure, some object – God is not a member of any class of being at all. The proper response to the ineffable, transcending love of God is awe, silence and contemplative ritual. Rowan had no glib answers to the problems of human tragedy and suffering. A disciple of the bleak and chastening novels of Dostoevsky and the theology of MacKinnon, he believed that the best a Christian can do is look at the full depth of human suffering and evil with a clear eye, and fall back only on faith and hope that this is not God's last word. This was why Rowan was reticent to chatter on about God as if he met him on a regular basis, and why he was so good with the prisoners at Grendon.

Rowan's talent was, like that of a poet, to make the strange familiar and the familiar strange. It was why he could never be pinned down and why, in a way, his enterprise was so admirable, inspiring and wise. But unlike the women in Kendal, he couldn't make it connect with ordinary lives. Rowan's theology and his speeches couldn't change the world as it was – just the way we look at it, and only for a while. Like Narnia – which he adored – he offered a land where you spend a delightful season, but from which you have to return to the real world with a bump.

Rowan's failure to inspire more widely lay not just in the obscurity of what he said, but in the very attempt to lead with words. The most popular spiritual leaders of the age, like the Dalai Lama or, within the Anglican Church, Desmond Tutu, led by who they were and how they related to people, all illuminated with carefully chosen gestures. After the Jeffrey John fiasco that route was closed to Rowan.

His instinct that spirituality could save the Church was nevertheless correct. Insofar as there were pockets of growth, they were where people found a deep sense of connection with something beyond ordinary life – in the silence of an empty church, the beauty of a sung evensong, the ecstasy of charismatic experience, the gift of healing, the flowers and stones of England. Insofar as he remained popular, especially with the Harry Potter generation, Rowan did so to the extent that he embodied something of this – a real-life Dumbledore complete with beard and robes.

But Rowan was completely defeated by the Ministry of Magic – the bureaucratic machinations of church bodies. If archbishops had been allowed to concentrate on their role as symbolic figures in the national pantomime, it might not have been so bad. Unfortunately they are also meant to run things. Rowan had neither the talent nor the inclination to do so. And into the power vacuum he created, came people who did.

One of the most effective was the Church's chief bureaucrat, William Fittall. Previously a civil servant to the government, he had succeeded the more old-school Philip Mawer. Mawer had endeavoured to steer the various warring bodies and factions of the Church towards something approximating a general good. Mr Fittall was a more focused and divisive figure, with a clearer party allegiance of his own. He was a lay reader and organist at St Mark's, Battersea Rise, the early HTB plant whose vicar, Paul Perkin, had close links with GAFCON and other groupings of conservatives intent on creating a gay-free, Bible-believing church within the church.

In post, Mr Fittall had a role not only in Church House, but also in the General Synod, Lambeth Palace, the House of Bishops and the Archbishops' Council. The changes introduced under Carey with the intention of centralizing power created a new opportunity. William Fittall was the one person who not only knew what was going on across the board but had agenda-setting and policy-drafting power. He also played a role in beefing up the Church's communications department, which began to issue increasingly upbeat summaries about the Church in the teeth of all evidence.

Another influential player in the vacuum left by Rowan was the Archbishops' Secretary for Appointments, Caroline Boddington. She belonged to a new generation of church bureaucrats: not old-style civil service, but new-style commercial-managerial, drafted in after Turnbull. With a background in the HR department at British Gas, she exercised power from the Wash House – the personnel department based in Lambeth Palace's former laundry.

The influence of the appointments secretary had always been significant, because the process worked with such secrecy that he or she had considerable room for manoeuvre. There was endless speculation about the list of names to be considered for preferment – a sort of clerical Book of Life, which was said to exist alongside a Book of Death that listed the names of unsuitables. But the power of the post swelled after 2007 when Gordon Brown (a son of the manse) sloughed off the remaining vestiges of Prime Ministerial involvement in appointments. This removed the need for a Prime Minister's Appointments Secretary – a full-time senior civil servant located in Downing Street, who brought to bear an important, extra-ecclesiastical perspective – and severed an important human link between Church and State. In practice it meant the removal of William Chapman, a civil servant who had helped draw up lists for the appointment of senior clergy since 1999, and had made it his business to find out about candidates and offer an independent perspective. Ironically, his departure made it more likely that partnered gay bishops would unwittingly be appointed.

A further complication was added when the Secretary for Appointments married the diocesan bishop who also happened to be a prominent member of the Church's Development and Appointments Group. With the key officer and a key member of the body which proposed candidates for senior preferment in the Church now married to one another, it became dangerous to offend or criticize either one.

The result was a drift towards the appointment of bishops of the 'safe rather than sorry' variety, managerially competent, and forever on message. Dissent and open debate dried up, and the long line of colourful Anglican bishops like David Jenkins – or Rowan – came to an abrupt end. Ensuring that there would never be another David Jenkins had been one of the aims of the Carey years. It's tempting to ask whether the successful policies of those years did more damage than the failures. Men who were completely normal by the standards of the House of Bishops could be remarkably off-putting to outsiders.

Increasingly, the House of Bishops appeared to be a mutual-support society, turned in on itself. Here Rowan retained his support. The House remained loyal, unwilling to contradict or disbelieve, even when they knew they were heading for yet another disaster. They stuck by him as every one of his major initiatives fell flat on its face. The revamped PR department, anxious to present a show of harmony and wholesomeness, reinforced the illusion. The mantra of unity was chanted more loudly to drive the demons away.

Yet far from making things more efficient, the ongoing rationalization of the power centres of the Church seemed to have little impact on its sclerotic decision-making capabilities, extreme aversion to risk, and labyrinthine processes and procedures. The extreme difficulty of ever getting a clear answer to anything persisted.

Linda experienced this slow-motion torture at first-hand when she proposed, as part of a national debate series she founded with Charles Clarke, the former Home Secretary, a conversation between Tony Blair and Rowan Williams on the place of religion in public life. She and Charles were invited to Lambeth Palace, where they faced an array of Palace staff arranged stiffly on the other side of the table like an interview committee. They presented their ideas and left, naively expecting that they would get a yes or no answer. Little did they know that they had embarked on a year-long series of negotiations, some of them fractious, about how, why and whether Rowan might actually take part. 'Haven't we established our bona fides by now?' Charles kept exclaiming in exasperation. 'I've never known anything like it.'

The discussions and conditions were extraordinary. Hours and hours were spent on the phone dealing with the Palace. Linda was deemed unsuitable to chair the debate on the explicit grounds that she was not of appropriate stature. Other possible candidates were chewed over somewhere in the bowels of Lambeth before being spat out as unsuitable. Hidden risks seemed to lurk everywhere. Eventually an acceptable candidate – Charles Moore – was found.

Every aspect of the event itself was discussed in the same gruelling detail, every jot and tittle had to be taken away for discussion and approval. The final showdown came on the day itself, when a plan to play Steve Harley's 'Make me Smile' as the audience left was intercepted by Palace staff and vetoed on the grounds that the lyrics had not been vetted – and that it was in any case insufficiently dignified for the Archbishop.

By contrast, Tony Blair had responded to the invitation to take part by return (and free of charge), and his office had no further involvement in the planning, trusting the organizers to get on with it.

As the Church's central bodies creaked on, increasingly isolated, defensive and concerned with their own introverted agendas, it became ever more apparent that the people of England had drifted away.

At the time that Runcie was Archbishop, it was still perfectly normal to be CofE. By the end of Rowan's time in office it was increasingly odd. It was no longer something people 'just were' and 'just did' because their parents and grandparents had; because they had been christened; because weddings and funerals were automatically church affairs; because people were in broad sympathy with the Church's outlook and values; because they trusted it; because they were English. The ties between Church and people had stretched and snapped, and all that was left of establishment was a constitutional husk. The shrivelled residue of Church–State relations remained, but the warm blood of Church–society relations had largely drained away.

Rowan's time as Archbishop coincided with that in which Britain moved decisively from being a Christian country to being a far more diverse but increasingly religiously unaffiliated one. By 2013, the year in which Rowan returned to academic life, the British Social Attitudes survey reported for the first time a majority of British people identifying not as Christian but as having 'no religion'. The proportion of 'nones' was highest among younger age groups, and the increase had been almost entirely at the expense of the Church of England.

But the 'nones' were not straightforwardly secular: they just didn't like organized religion. Linda's surveys found that fewer than half of those who reported 'no religion' were atheists, and only a small fraction were hostile to religion in the manner of Richard Dawkins. A quarter took part in some regular spiritual activity – like prayer. RE became the fastest-growing subject in schools, and the attitude of younger people changed. When Linda first started teaching eighteen-year-olds about religion in the early 1990s, their exam answers to questions about secularization defaulted back to narratives about the rise of science driving religion from the scene. By the start of the new millennium, that background narrative had been wholly replaced by one about the eclipse of traditional organized forms of religion by new, more diverse forms of spirituality and non-religion. Students were less prejudiced against Christianity, but more ignorant. They were increasingly likely to have been brought up with no living contact with the churches besides what they saw in the media and learned at school.

Spirituality of the kind Rowan and Stephen Sykes disliked had become ever more mainstream and ever less overtly religious. It eased its way into schools, hospitals, leisure activities and the media. Activities like yoga, meditation, mindfulness and Tai Chi ceased to seem exotic and counter-cultural and became part of everyday English life, prescribed on the NHS or recommended by a friend. Words like 'chi', 'holistic', 'spiritual development' and 'Energy' with a capital 'E' became commonplace terms, while Christian concepts became alien – the BBC News website could style a being it had obviously never encountered before 'a "reverent"'.

The retreat of the CofE to the margins of society was nowhere more evident than in the decline of its role in hatching, matching and dispatching English people of every rank and station.

This was partly the fault of its own moralizing. As one clergyman observed in the *Church Times*, the Church had become the only organization for which the customer is always wrong. Ignoring the fact that English people had a historic entitlement to be baptized, married and buried by 'their' church, some more zealous clergy had started insisting on conditions before people could get married or have a child baptized, causing much offence and hurt in the process. The Church's long-standing opposition to divorce and remarriage was particularly damaging, especially as remarriages grew to become almost as common as first marriages, and venues other than churches were licensed for weddings. The fact that the Church in Rowan's time was backtracking on this opposition was too little too late. By 2013, two-thirds of marriages were civil ones, only a third religious. The CofE performed just one in five.

Many people simply wanted more choice and involvement. As the Church lost its grip over the provision of ceremonies, the English – always great ritual innovators – took to the task of reinventing them with relish. The early twenty-first century saw the introduction of pregnancy rituals, baby showers, baby-naming ceremonies, high school proms, engagement ceremonies, lavish stag parties and hen nights, divorce parties, and a plethora of new practices around death, burial and the disposal of ashes. Large numbers reported wanting 'less funereal' funerals. 'Non-religious' funerals – civil, green and humanist – grew to meet the demand. Ironically, a large proportion of the celebrants who took market share from the Church were Anglican or ex-Anglican women. In more hospitable circumstances they, like their mothers and grandmothers before them, would have been serving the Church, not competing with it.

None of this was inevitable. The Church of England's closest counterparts, the historic state churches of Denmark, Norway and Sweden, retained much higher levels of public trust and commitment. People continued to turn to them at pivotal moments of life and death. Although they experienced similarly sharp declines in Sunday churchgoing as the Church of England, they retained their deep insertion points into wider society. Church, state and society kept in step with one another. The most successful Scandinavian churches had started ordaining women not long after the Second World War, had accepted gay people, and when same-sex marriage became legal had offered it. Levels of baptism, confirmation, weddings and funerals remained high.

So the most remarkable thing was not how much progress rational secularism made during the period covered by this book, but how little. As late as the 1980s, it had seemed quite reasonable to imagine that religion would wither away to the point where it had no influence on politics or public life at home or abroad. By the new millennium, it was clear that this had been a false prophecy: religion was more visible and influential than ever, and it was secular utopian hopes and dreams of post-war political paradises which had been defeated – from Kiev to Cairo.

Archbishops could go on blaming 'secularization' for church decline, but even in Britain the reality was more complex. It wasn't just that people had come adrift from the churches, the churches had come adrift from them.

On the whole the English had never been very religious. At least since the Civil War, religious enthusiasm unnerved and embarrassed them. They preferred a cool relationship to their religious and political institutions. Rioting and revolution was for the French, and religious enthusiasm for Americans. If you ask English people how religious they are the vast majority, including those who are Christian, say they are 'not religious'. Older people are as likely to say it as younger. But the Church of England post-Runcie had been becoming increasingly inhospitable to the not-very-religious English, demanding more of its 'followers' than occasional attendance, and drawing an ever sharper line between 'real' Anglicans and 'nominal' ones. Weekly Sunday-morning churchgoing became the expectation rather than the exception, partly because of the pressing need to raise money from the pews, and partly because of the growing influence of the evangelical model of a gathered, congregational church rather than a societal one.

But by now it was clear that insofar as evangelical Anglicanism had succeeded it had done so by becoming 'niche'. In the terminology of evolutionary biology, it flourished in very specific fitness environments: university cities where it could run a lively, large church for students, and middle-class parishes where it could cater to affluent families. With its close ties to the social elites of London and the home counties, its wealth and superb organization, HTB grew to become its most successful brand and franchise. During the Rowan years, it extended its reach through modular training courses for laity and clergy and its simple and clear message to follow Jesus, receive the Spirit, join a lively church, get married, and pass on the message with indefatigable enthusiasm. No wonder it sometimes felt it had God in its pocket. As an intercessor in HTB once began a prayer: 'And finally, Lord, regarding the General Election ...' While the rest of the Church agonized about mission initiatives, HTB just got on and did it.

Yet evangelical success wasn't enough to register as even a pimple on the steady chart of decline. Affiliation, membership and church attendance all continued to fall relentlessly. By the end of Rowan's time, regular churchgoing had fallen to less than 2 per cent of the general population, and the average attender was elderly.

Churchgoing had never attracted a majority of English people, but the brand of Sunday-morning worship available to them in most Anglican churches in the twenty-first century proved particularly unappealing to a society with a low boredom threshold and high production values. Children and young people shifted miserably in their seats or played with smartphones, and even adults struggled to retain interest. No amount of liturgical revision could help: it just added more words. Only the ritualist Anglo-Catholics and the charismatics took seriously the problem of boredom and tried to construct services which, in their very different styles, offered something which transcended everyday experience.

A very good sermon could ease the boredom, but these were few and far between. Conservative evangelical ones were usually straight biblical exegesis, like a dull and sporadically hectoring lecture with no opportunity for questions. Charismatic evangelical ones delivered biblical verses and personal anecdotes in numbered points designed to leave no doubt that a personal relationship with Jesus would improve your life. And liberal ones found a hundred and one ways to tell you to love your neighbour and deplore the individualism of the wider society which was happily eating brunch somewhere else while thinking materialist thoughts. Whatever the churchmanship, there was a likelihood one would hear about the God-shaped hole which gapes in society and can only be filled by coming to church more often.

While the CofE Communications department put a brave spin on all this, the evidence on the ground was increasingly hard to ignore. Some smaller congregations were literally starting to die out. Rural churches were being grouped into ever-larger 'multiple benefices' with exhausted clergy driving endlessly from one to the next, and urban churches overall were faring even more disastrously than rural ones. A tendency to neglect the parts of the Church which had long been the strongest (older women, rural churches) in favour of those which were never as successful (young men, urban churches) grew more pronounced, as did the desire to nurture true-believing disciples and ditch Laodicean 'culture Christians' along with their Erastian expectations of church, state and society acting in reasonable harmony. 'The Church would look a lot more attractive', suggested Monica Furlong, 'if it was not continually yearning, like a neglected lover, over those who stay away. It could try celebrating the clientele it has got.'

Unlike Runcie and even Carey, Rowan had little feeling for the gods of the English. For him, real religion had nothing to do with sacred practices around tea-urns, village fetes and flower-rotas. To the extent that the Church was bound up with Jane Austen and John Betjeman, cabbage roses and cakes, *Daily Mail* readers and Waitrose shoppers, he eschewed it. He was a 'hairy leftie' and proud of it, but a majority of Anglicans still voted Conservative. Rowan's heart was in Wales, where he had been born and raised, and to which he returned as bishop of Monmouth. He had the sensibility of a non-conformist, a rebel and outsider, not a member of the Establishment. At root, he remained Anglo-Catholic: deeply churchy, clerical, spiritual and other-worldly.

Rowan's stance was reinforced by the theological trends of the time, which were programmatically 'post-liberal' and 'post-Christendom'. The latter sought to sever remaining ties between church and worldly power, so that a pure gospel free from secular contamination could emerge. The overall idea, stemming from Karl Barth's 'dialectical theology' and H. Richard Niebuhr's *Christ and Culture* updated with a dose of Alasdair MacIntyre (born an Ulster Protestant, converted first to Marxism then Roman Catholicism – always an outsider), was that Christians must not collude with state and society, but 'confess' against them. To this was added a big dollop of cultural pessimism, a heady sense of cultural rebellion, and an unspoken nostalgia for a time when dons and clergy were held in higher esteem.

'Post-liberalism' involved a rejection of liberal theology and a distaste for societies like Britain and the USA which were considered to be captive to unsustainable ideas of individual freedom and self-fulfilment, lacking true virtues and the religious communities which nurtured them. Symptomatic of their fallen state was said to be the fact that they weren't taking theology seriously – a rather self-fulfilling prophecy. Stanley Hauerwas, the bombastic Texan doyen of this school, wrote books with martial titles like *Dispatches from the Front*, where the enemy seemed to include Walmart and Oprah Winfrey. He argued that the Christian narrative could only be truthfully told from within the counter-cultural space of tight church congregations engaged in a war against the individualistic, uncaring selfishness of liberal society.

It was one thing to conclude that the world was the enemy of the Church. That in itself would have been something to shake a societal church such as the Church of England had once been. But if you're going to make the world your enemy, you need to know it. That had been one of the traditional strengths of a clergy caste recruited from the Establishment: the ones who took the world for their enemy had been to school with its leaders and knew their weaknesses. But the theological turn from 'the world' was compounded by a refusal to understand it. The English theologian John Milbank argued that social theory was a sneaky kind of anti-theological secular metaphysics dressed up as science. This theological rationale, combined with a genuine lack of interest in ordinary Anglicans and how society actually functions, deprived Rowan and the Church of another channel which might have kept them in closer touch with reality. The fragmentation, the loneliness and the anomie of the modern rich world was contrasted in the post-liberal imagination with the courage and community spirit of the poor. This thought is common across almost all forms of contemporary Christianity except those that are actually growing fastest in the poor world: the magical and greedy strains of Pentecostalism which promise wealth as well as healing to the believer. But 'Blessed are the poor in spirit', said Jesus, and this is a constant theme in papal encyclicals. It does something to explain the sense of obligation towards some African churches which marked Rowan's struggles in the Anglican Communion, and it was these struggles which took up increasing amounts of the Archbishop's time.

Once Rowan had shown he could be bullied, the conservatives redoubled their efforts to enforce a homophobic line across all the churches of the Anglican Communion. Conservatives of course hate the term 'homophobia', and it cannot be fairly applied to all of them. Rowan himself did not have any aversion to gay people, as we've seen. He just thought that the interests of honest gay clergy were less important and urgent than those of their opponents. You could quite sanely argue that the well-being of poor African Christians should take precedence over the job prospects of rich English ones. Other opponents of gay equality simply took their colour from the changing society around them and could be relied on to change their minds approximately ten years after the majority of society had done so.

But many of the opponents, and the ones who cared most, really and fairly could be described as homophobic. The logic of the ghastly Lambeth Conference of 1998 still operated; the memory of the attempted exorcism of Richard Kirker lingered on. The drunken English bishop cheerfully reciting 'I thank you Lord, that I am not a fairy ...' at the same conference had spoken for a number of his peers. There were also practical and material advantages to the African churches if homophobia could be established as the test of orthodoxy within the Communion, particularly for the

Nigerian, Ugandan and Rwandan ones, all of which set up foreign subsidiaries to exploit the situation. They hoped it would open up lucrative export opportunities among disaffected congregations. A number of American conservatives, and a few English ones, set up as bishops or advisers to these African churches and ran their policies towards the official Anglican churches back home.

In the middle of this snakepit stood Rowan, talking as if words still meant anything. At successive meetings of the Primates of the Anglican Communion he attempted to work out a compromise by which the liberals would stop doing what they believed in, and the conservatives would stop saying what they believed. One in particular, at Dromantine in Northern Ireland, showed what he was up against. The official communiqué when it was all over contained the following sentences: 'We continue unreservedly to be committed to the pastoral support and care of homosexual people. The victimisation or diminishment of human beings whose affections happen to be ordered towards people of the same sex is anathema to us. We assure homosexual people that they are children of God, loved and valued by him, and deserving of the best we can give of pastoral care and friendship.' But outside the conference hall the Nigerian primate Peter Akinola was heard on his mobile phone talking to an American adviser about Rowan, saying, 'He'll do anything we tell him to.' Sure enough, the rest of the communiqué set in motion a process which would have resulted in the expulsion of the liberal provinces. What stopped it was the discovery that there was no mechanism for doing so.

The Anglican Communion turned out to exist, organizationally, only in the mind of the Archbishop of Canterbury. His plan to rescue something from the shambles was that all the churches involved would promise to stick to the rules they had agreed. This was formalized in the idea of an 'Anglican Covenant'. 'Covenant' is church-speak for a contract between a lesser power – like ancient Israel or the churches of the Anglican Communion, and a greater one – like God or the Archbishop of Canterbury. The idea was that all the various parts of the Communion would voluntarily surrender some degree of autonomy in order to live peacefully together under the guiding wisdom of Canterbury. Since no participating church had anything whatsoever to gain on the issue of homosexuality by yielding to its opponents, the idea never stood a chance. It had been obvious ever since the attempted exorcism of Kirker that the liberal churches would not do what the conservatives ordered, and the conservatives thought the liberal prescription was satanic. None the less, Rowan seems to have believed that the Church of England would happily give the Church of Nigeria a vote in the Church of England's own internal deliberations, and spent years campaigning for the scheme. He even made a YouTube video to plead for it. The plan got as far as being referred for formal consideration round the English dioceses, where it was rejected.

After it became obvious that Rowan would not make any serious attempt to expel the liberal North Americans, many of the African and a few Asian churches, along with the Calvinist evangelicals of the almost independent diocese of Sydney, formed their own global organization, originally under the unfortunate acronym of FOCA – the 'Fellowship of Confessing Anglicans', a name which was meant to link them to the 'Confessing Churches' that resisted Nazi rule in Germany. It was this which later became 'GAFCON', the Global

Anglican Futures Conference. It was able to draw the bishops and archbishops who would otherwise have attended the 2008 Lambeth Conference to a rival meeting in Jerusalem.

Back in Britain, the wrangling had ceased to make much of an impression on the general public. The trouble over women bishops did. The decision to admit women to the priesthood, taken in 1992, had not made provision for women bishops. This odd half-measure was dreamt up as a way to respect the 'integrity' of the different sides in the battle, but a diversity which excluded those who believed in the full equality of women could not last. To overthrow that compromise, however, would require another round of legislation, in the Synod and then in Parliament. So the battle for women's equality in the Church had to be waged all over again. The Movement for the Ordination of Women rolled up its sleeves like Rosie the Riveter, rebranded itself as WATCH ('women and the church'), and got to work. So did opponents, although this time round the real fervour, and the numbers, came not from Anglo-Catholics but from conservative evangelicals who believed that the Bible mandated patriarchy.

In theory, Rowan was supportive of women bishops. But his desire to achieve that end was dwarfed by his desire to get there through widespread agreement, with no clergyman left behind.

The debates rolled on interminably, even after the conservative groups admitted that the theological argument had been lost. It had become much more a matter of identity politics and how various party interests could be served and face could be saved. How were those who did not want women bishops or their oversight to be protected and compensated? At stake was the fundamental principle of an episcopal church that the bishop is a symbol of unity. But as with 'flying bishops' before, opponents wanted 'alternative oversight'. Rowan and the House of Bishops proposed and tinkered about with so many pieces of morally and theologically inadequate compromise legislation that Synod lost trust, and everyone lost patience. By the time it finally came to a vote in 2012, the tempers of Synod members were badly frayed.

The goal, Rowan continued to insist, must be to preserve the highest degree of unity in the Church of England and beyond. Even after two decades of arguing, he maintained that there still needed to be more 'sustained and prayerful reflection' until the 'risk of mutual isolation' could be overcome.

His state of mind is revealed by the suggestion that the Church was actually doing something exemplary in failing to come to agreement over this issue of basic equality which other institutions in British society had settled decades before. Rather than representing a failure of moral and theological nerve, the process might, he mused, be 'beginning to model something for the Church Catholic and the world at large. Integrity need not mean absolute division; it can mean a process of admittedly painful, often untidy, but finally deeply evangelical self-discovery, the discovery of what God purposes for us.'

If England had nodded off by the time the vote finally came to be taken in General Synod, the news that the proposal to allow women bishops had failed to attain the necessary majority among the laity shocked into wakefulness almost everyone who could remember what the Church of England was. Even the Prime Minister David Cameron was moved to make a statement in the House of Commons saying that 'They need to get on with it, as it were, and get with the programme.'

The debacle over women bishops was a perfect symbol not only of Rowan's failure to get a grip on things, but of the yawning gulf which had opened between the people of England and the Church of England. Urgent questions were asked. Private Members Bills were threatened. There were private meetings between Parliamentarians and senior clergy. To the general public, it sent as clear a message as could be that the Church was on another planet.

Rowan, who had already decided to resign as Archbishop, stepped down just a few days later.

# 11

# The inheritors

Sometime towards the end of Rowan's period of office, Andrew was invited to preach, or at least to talk, at an Oxbridge College, where the chaplain was an ambitious and thoughtful man who had worked under several regimes at Lambeth Palace. Talking afterwards, the chaplain said that the Church of England now felt like the last days of East Germany: no one believes the public myth, but there is nothing to put in its place. The worse things got, the more the Church pumped out cheery propaganda. 'We're all just waiting for the wall to fall,' he said.

He wasn't, of course, talking about Christianity. There really is no good reason now to be a priest in the Church of England if you don't take Christianity seriously. But the institution, the establishment of the Church, really had come to seem a vast, moth-eaten musical brocade. In the thirty years covered by this book the old parties, indeed the old structures, had consumed themselves and each other.

The liberals and the dons had been robbed of power under George Carey and then robbed of hope by their supposed leader Rowan Williams. The evangelicals achieved power and then showed they had no idea what to do with it, themselves splintering into contending factions. The Anglo-Catholics were smashed to bits by feminism. All that seemed left was worried clergy and ageing congregations huddled in decaying buildings with a kind of grey determination to keep up the show. A rural vicar's wife said to Andrew, quite without irony, that things would be so much easier if they could get younger laypeople involved – and by younger, she explained, she meant those in their fifties rather than their seventies.

The East German metaphor was so memorable because it felt so true. Yet, just as in East Germany, things didn't feel too bad at the human level. One of the enduring mysteries of the Church of England is how many thoughtful, energetic and realistic people gave their lives to an institution that is now none of these things.

One particularly important example came from the diocese of Durham, where one strand of this story began. The figure of David Jenkins, The Bishop Who Didn't Believe A Word Of It, had loomed over the Church at the start of this tale. It had been an explicit aim of George Carey's time as Archbishop to ensure that no one like him was ever appointed a bishop again. This policy had not produced the anticipated outcome: Jenkins' immediate successor, Michael Turnbull, was largely occupied with internal Church reform; he was in turn succeeded by an evangelical scholar of entirely conventional sexuality and so much energy and self-importance that at the launch of one of his books, an 800-page doorstop on St Paul, he spoke for forty minutes, oblivious to the growing discomfort and incredulity of his audience.

His successor, Justin Welby, found a diocese in fairly desperate straits. He told his Bishop's Council: 'Big buildings and big institutions fall down slowly, but there comes a point when the roof really does fall in, [then] we move from being Durham Cathedral to Fountains Abbey ... My own gut feeling is that there will be serious questions of viability before I retire, probably camouflaged in pastoral reorganizing at diocesan level. Say seven to ten years.' This was what evangelicals, including George Carey, had been saying for decades, to encourage lively evangelism. But one got the sense with Welby that he believed it.

Between 1989 and 2010 Durham had lost just under a third of its adult attenders (in the same period, Liverpool, Lincoln and Blackburn had all lost more than a third of their attenders but Durham was the sixth worst in the country by this measure). A quarter of the running costs were being met by the Church Commissioners, and more than a third of the parishes did not pay their assessed share of diocesan costs in full. To withhold quota payments as a way of putting pressure on the liberals had thirty years before been the threat, the hope and finally the established practice of conservative evangelical churches, but this was something much wider and more threatening. Parishes were failing to pay not as part of a political strategy but because their congregations really felt they could not afford it. We are 'near the tipping point at which any PCC will be tempted to hold back since so many others appear to do so', the incoming bishop warned.

His solution was a blend of honesty and arm-twisting: parishes could set their own quota, based on what they honestly believed they could pay – but once they had set a figure, they must stick to it, and those which failed to pay their share could expect a loss of stipendiary clergy. Whether this will work we don't know. Welby had moved on before the results were in. But at least he had looked the dragons in the eye.

Justin Welby had been formed by Holy Trinity Brompton, and remained part of this church within the Church. He had been at Eton and Cambridge with Nicky Gumbel and was in many ways entirely typical of that milieu. One side of the family was old posh: his mother had been Churchill's personal secretary and her second marriage was to a peer; the other conspicuously rich: his father was a businessman who had made a mysterious fortune in America. He himself became a successful executive in an oil company. He married the sister of one of the secretaries at HTB (Sandy Millar had given him a discreet steer in her direction when he went up to Cambridge). All this looked entirely conventional, and exactly as HTB expected. But underneath there were darker currents. His parents divorced and his father took to the bottle and died broke. Only once he was dead did Welby discover that Welby Senior had actually been a German Jew who had made his first fortune bootlegging in America in the 1930s. Still later, the journalist Charles Moore discovered and proved that Welby's biological father had been someone else altogether. Welby's response was that biological parenthood didn't matter to him as his identity was rooted in Jesus Christ. Nor was his own family untroubled. The Welbys' first child died in a road accident while still a baby; a daughter has spoken publicly about her depression.

He entered the ministry late, and studied at Durham. He spent most of his time as a parish priest in a small town south of Coventry. The building he worked in was 700 years old. Southam was still overwhelmingly Christian by culture – more than 5,400 people called themselves Christians in the 2001 Census – but church attendance was a failing habit. That year the main Sunday service in Welby's church had an average attendance of eighty. This meant he had doubled the attendance since he arrived in 1995. But the long, slow ageing of the Church continued. By 2007, two-thirds of the regular attenders in the diocese were over fifty-five and nearly half were over sixty, while the pews in Southam were still in place.

After six years Welby moved back onto the HTB network, to Coventry Cathedral, where Andrew White, a former curate of Paul Perkin's at Battersea Rise, was running the international ministry of reconciliation. This in itself was a mark of the long march of HTB through the institutions: White's predecessor had been the German Quaker and *Guardian* writer Paul Oestreicher; White later moved to Baghdad after the American invasion and claimed to Andrew's wife that he talked to President George W. Bush on the phone every week. Oestreicher would have had different things to say in those conversations.

At Coventry, Welby took on an international role, working for reconciliation around the world. This meant a lot of travel to Anglican churches, but it was outside the disastrous and dysfunctional structures of the Anglican Communion and took place at a level far below official visits. On these trips he showed courage and dedication. He was held at gunpoint more often than any previous Archbishop and closer to a violent death than anyone since Runcie struggled through northern Europe in a tank regiment after D-Day. He paid more than a hundred visits to Nigeria: one consequence was that though he loved the country he had fewer illusions about its Anglican Church than many English evangelicals.

Welby made deep connections with Roman Catholics – his spiritual director is a Roman Catholic priest – without any of the old hope of corporate reunion. The Welby family also maintained intimate connections with the Vineyard movement on the charismatic edge of American Christianity: it was a Vineyard pastor who comforted them after the death of their first child.

So the question arises: what was a man of such energy doing in the Church of England? While it might be explained as part of the mystery of a church full of intelligent, thoughtful, humble and hard-working people which works against all these qualities when it is considered as an organization, in the case of Justin Welby the answer was also that he did not think he was working for the Church of England at all. Like others in the HTB group, he thought he was working for Jesus. The Church of England was merely a vehicle.

This needs some unpacking. The contemporary evangelical fondness for Jesus is something that makes other people – including other Anglicans – back away, inconspicuously if they can, rudely if they must. For Christians who don't want community, who shrink from the exchange of greetings at the Peace, and who don't like imposing their beliefs on others, banging on about Jesus is horrible. In the wider world it just marks you as weird. So it's another mystery why evangelicals, who are supposed to be interested in conversion, wear all their most unattractive characteristics on the outside. The answer is that Jesus means from the inside something entirely different: the place and source of life, support and guidance. To talk about Jesus, in this sense, is something like talking about music, if music were a person who loved and understood you. It's only ghastly for people who don't hear it from the inside.

There's a more profound point as well, which is that to other Anglicans all the talk of Jesus sounds sectarian. Unlike 'God' or 'Spirit', it sharply distinguishes those who use it from other kinds of churchmanship, as well as from other religions. This boundary-marking is, of course, deliberate, for it supports a congregational rather than a societal vision of what the Church should be.

From Coventry, Welby went to Liverpool Cathedral as Dean, where he showed a gift for PR by having the cathedral bells ring out John Lennon's atheist dirge 'Imagine'. This did a lot more for Christianity than preaching against it might have accomplished. From Liverpool he moved to Durham, as bishop, and he had only been there nine months before he was chosen for Canterbury. He had had even less experience as a diocesan bishop than Carey. But in the twilight of the Rowan years, the Church Commissioners started to look much harder at church statistics. The answers were phenomenally bleak. If present trends continued, there would be only 150,000 churchgoing Anglicans left in England by 2050.

The only one of the shortlisted candidates to take this entirely seriously was Justin Welby. Other candidates who might have done so were ruled out for various reasons: Richard Chartres because of his equivocal attitude to women clergy; John Sentamu for his autocratic style. Welby combined a reputation for managerial competence with self-deprecating charm and worldly wisdom. When he moved to the lectern in Lambeth Palace, a spare and ascetic figure dressed all in black, the head of PR for HTB could be seen watching from the sidelines. The long march through the Church of England had finally ended for them. Their man was in post. But what was now left of the institution they had marched through?

Things could not go on. Everyone saw that at last. How could they be changed? There were – there are – a number of possible ways things might unfold from here, and all of them are rooted in aspects of the story we have told.

The long, slow movements all continued and all will, so far as we can see, continue for the foreseeable future: the drift of the institutional church away from its anchorings in national life; the change from funding by the endowments of dead Christians to funding by live ones; the shrinking of lay involvement, including Parliamentary involvement in church affairs. All these continued to push the Church of England ever further from the historic national model still taken for granted by the men who had met in Windsor Castle only thirty years previously. And, now, everyone understands that it will never get back there and can no longer afford to attempt the impossible.

The story we have told is of an England which has changed too much, and of a national church which has changed too little. Some took refuge in the idea that the Church was standing as a 'prophetic witness' against a secular age, which was more comforting than admitting that it was stuck in the 1950s. The alternative defence, that the Church couldn't embrace moral advances like the equal treatment of women and of gay people without agonizing for decades, was much weaker. At their best, churches have led moral change, not lagged behind it, as with civil rights or anti-slavery. Surveys revealed that rank-and-file Anglicans had embraced these shifts long before their leaders caught up.

But the pace and scale of change would have damaged the Church whatever it had done. National churches everywhere were challenged by the fundamental fact that the nation was no longer the focus of patriotism, ethnic solidarity and sacred sentiment it once had been. In Britain the immediate post-war and early Cold War period was the last time people really felt this way. Thereafter, increasing religious and secular diversity, experienced as proliferating possibilities of identity, created a severe problem for a church designed to serve everyone with a single product. This was compounded by the way in which people became linked across cyberspace rather than by local association and national imagining. By the time Tony Blair took office, Britain had become diverse, non-deferential, liberal and participatory, while its church still clung to ideals of unity, common good and 'one size fits all'.

But even when compared with its closest historical cousins, the churches of Denmark, Norway and Sweden, the Church of England did worse. In 2014 two-thirds of Danes were still baptized by their national church, in England the figure was nearer one in ten; in Denmark four-fifths of people had a church funeral, in England only a third; in Denmark over three-quarters of the population were paying members of the Church, in England fewer than 2 per cent. Only Sunday church attendance approached the same low levels in Denmark as in England: as a committed societal church this worried the Church of Denmark far less. Unlike the Church of England, however, the Scandinavian churches are funded through the state, so that it is not active churchgoers who pay for them but anyone who wants the Church to be there if they ever need it.

As we have seen, the CofE compounded its difficulties by either ignoring or denouncing what was happening, and by taking refuge in voodoo – in empty gestures of managerialism, fantasies about global Anglican unity, rhetoric and PR. Unlike the other great public institutions of post-war Britain, the Church was shielded from the need to change by great wealth well managed, apathy on the part of Parliament, and the simple fact that the bruised, frustrated and dissatisfied could much more easily leave than change anything.

This was the most tragic loss during the decades of decline charted in this book: that ordinary Anglicans – of whom there were still several million – who cared for the Church, wanted to help, and were increasingly well qualified to do so, were squeezed out by structures and stalling. They found, sometimes to their regret, that the only way to exercise their spiritual gifts, other than by being ordained, was to leave. And once people find they can become spiritual adults on their own terms, they are rather unlikely to go back.

So can anything last, and how might the Church survive and even grow?

Much depends on the environment in which it will operate. One possibility, of course, is that secularism will become ascendant and that religion will disappear. That still seemed plausible in the early 1980s, but after 1989 and the fall of the Berlin Wall, the great secular hopes of the twentieth century fell away. Communism had failed to deliver, and the unfeeling cruelties of unregulated capitalism became ever clearer as the new millennium got underway. For new generations, religion and spirituality did not seem such a stupid place to look for guidance and inspiration in achieving wholeness or even holiness. It seems that the things that religions do, and the need for them, will never go away. People still seek healing, ritual, connection with their ancestors, and links with their descendants. They need community and some need explanations of their purpose in life. All of these need to be public if they are to be fully effective. Whatever fulfils those functions will be of interest to sociologists of religion, whether or not there is one single institution to carry them out, as there was under Christendom, and whatever it is called.

Nevertheless, the wider environment currently looks extremely hostile to any resurgence of old-style 'religion'. The word itself has become toxic. It now stands for authoritarian and occasionally violent obscurantism, for the oppression of women, and for old people trying to stop young ones getting laid. This is true of Islam as well as Christianity, but Islam is still sustained in Britain within the networks of extended families, and reinforced by a much greater level of hostility and prejudice from the outside world than Christians in Europe suffer. And the Christian churches, almost as much as the Muslim authorities, have played along with the negative stereotypes. Conservative elements within church leaderships, both Roman Catholic and Protestant, have since the early 1980s believed that liberals were their greatest enemies, blamed them for the failure of religion, and in this process tended to discredit liberal, moderate religion in the eyes of an increasingly liberal public as well. The idea that liberalism was a 'wishy washy' version of the true gospel was revealing; it conveniently forgot about the harsh political struggles by which first the unpropertied classes, then 'blacks', then women, children and gay people gradually won the same rights as gentlemen, and the role that Christians had played in these struggles.

There were places where the Church's traditional model was most obviously unsustainable. These were often those places where it once had worked best. The Church of England remains relatively more successful – or at any rate less unsuccessful – in the countryside than in cities, but country parishes, and their often wonderful buildings, are increasingly hard to sustain. In even worse straits are the Victorian barns which had been the glory of the Church a hundred years ago, and the hopeful brick and concrete churches of the 1950s. Less tangibly, the authority with which bishops had once seemed to speak has disappeared completely. All are now echoing and empty. The various forms of administration, from the Synod through to the archbishops' and bishops' palaces, are distrusted and ineffective. Managerial voodoo only made things worse.

One approach would be to abandon all those pretensions and turn the Church into a full-hearted congregational rather than societal arrangement, with no duties or ties to the wider, indifferent society around it. This would follow the logic of effective disestablishment. The Church would become one voluntary society among many, growing where it could be strong, and pulling back from markets where it had no chance of success. Central control would consist largely in a refusal to try to control and direct resources centrally. The Church Commissioners' role would be to pay for the upkeep of those buildings which could no longer be financially supported by their own congregations: that means almost all the buildings from before about 1900, including many cathedrals and just about every church that might ever appear in a tourist-board photograph. What would happen to church schools under such a scenario would depend on the government. But it seems obvious that the logic of effective disestablishment leads quickly to the real thing. In such a case, without either attractive and distinctive rituals and worship, or any anchoring in the rituals and history of a wider community, the Church of England would wither to become a marginal denomination. The spiritual energies and moral life of the nation would be diverted even more decisively into quite different channels.

A second would be to try and turn the Church into a single organization, capable of working coherently towards defined worldly goals. This would correspond to the picture of the Church which lurks in the background of much press coverage and senior clerics' minds: there are leaders, who decide what should be done, and followers, hierarchically arranged, who do it. It is financed by laypeople whose money is harvested by a caste of worker drone priests. This model is a constant temptation to archbishops, as we have seen. Yet it will always be a mirage. It may be possible to produce a disciplined and obedient priesthood, fearful of the sack, where the conditions of employment are much more as they are in the commercial world. It would certainly be possible to promote as bishops the most talented middle managers and let them manage middlingly. But all these arrangements would tend in themselves to alienate the increasingly well-educated and responsible laity on whom it all depends, and would remove the moral idealism and spiritual depth which makes religion attractive. The Church would be no more than a business run by clerical executives. If it does not provide at least the shadow of another, better world – what Christians call the Kingdom of Heaven – it will be an absolute failure. All of the most successful forms of religion in the world today are fantastically disorganized above the level of the single congregation, even when they are rigid in their doctrine; and all the popular forms of spirituality offer to open up new possibilities for life, not close them down.

Yet though both these approaches are doomed to failure, both of them grow out of real problems, and attempts to tackle them. The congregations do matter, since this is where the activists are, and they are the people who currently pay for the Church. Yet they have no power, except to leave. They can of course, and will, affect the Church by dying without replacement, but that is not a choice. Somehow they must be given a stake. So too must the much larger body of Anglicans who have a more distant relationship with the Church, but value it none the less. What the centralized, managerial vision realizes is that the job of the clergy is at present impossible. There are too many expectations pulling in too many directions. No one can say what constitutes success or often even failure, and over half of the clergy feel that their talents are not recognized or supported. That isn't workable either. Neither approach takes seriously the fact that church decline is largely the result of young people ceasing to follow their parents into the pew, or thinks hard about how children become Christians. And neither addresses the vast, life-giving penumbra of the Church: the people who want its services only occasionally, and have no need for the sort of regular community experience it offers. If they can see that the Church exists for them once again, they may well be persuaded to encourage their children that it's worthwhile, and help pay for it.

Both the empowerment of committed congregations and the increasing control and professionalization of the clergy tend to make religion weirder. It is as if transport policy were shaped by the interests of people who read motoring magazines, rather than those who merely drive. It is very difficult for an organization to understand that its role in many people's lives is to be boring and peripheral. They want it to be boring except when it is suddenly very moving indeed. Sermons are generally boring, unless they are preached at the funeral of someone you love.

One central underlying idea of this book has been that the Church of England is lost because the England of which it was the Church has disappeared. That England – the one whose ghost still lurks within the battlements of Windsor Castle – was run by a small caste of gentlemen leaders who were ultimately trained as infantry officers: men with practical organizational skills, who could look after their men and lead them to their deaths. They combined charisma with effectiveness. Neither they, nor their followers, are to be found today.

But even in an army, the visible, fighting troops are dependent on an enormous apparatus of supply and reinforcement. When the Church of England's priesthood was drawn from among men who might have been, and sometimes had been, officers, they were in turn dependent on a supply train of women. These were not followers, but part of the organization, even if unpaid and never officially recognized. They, too, have disappeared. The last generation is about to die.

All these roles still need filling. If there is no one person or type who can any longer fill them, the answer must be to split them into different jobs. The parish priest can no longer function as a manager, a leader, a provider of pastoral care and a spiritual figure.

The laity are no longer content simply to be followers, and to supply the money with no choice in how or why it is used. The managerial and organizational roles should be filled by well-qualified and properly paid laity. If managers are paid solely for organizing, and the demand for them is judged by those organized, it is astonishing how few will be needed. Leadership is probably not a role that any one person should have, especially in religion. The evangelical model of ministry teams, where laity and clergy work in a genuine partnership, is one of the greatest reasons for their success, and far more significant than the theology. Even pastoral care needs be done very largely by the laity: this is what following Jesus means in practice to many of those who still care a lot about it.

Clergy have become expensive, and full-time paid ones should be treated as scarce resources for jobs only they can do. Stipendiary priests will then be freed to do what they can do best, not what laity can do better and cheaper – and that will probably be something for which there is no space in the secular world at the moment. Clergy who support themselves through their own jobs in the 'real world' must become the norm, and cease to be treated like second-class citizens by the Church. This will not only save an awful lot of money; it will end the unreality of the present conditions of clergy housing and remuneration, which cause difficulties for clergy families, and create an unnecessary distance between their lives and those of everyone else.

If what survives is to be the church of a new England (the old one having disappeared) it has to be a church for England, and not for the Church: in the years of voodoo, the effort was all put into rescuing and strengthening the institution, especially at the centre, as if that were the only thing which mattered. The Synod was the ultimate expression of that sentiment, though it started as a compromised and half-hearted attempt to do the opposite and bring ordinary England into the decision-making of the Church. England is far more diverse now than when this book opened, and the failure of the Church has, in part, been its failure to deal with diversity, including its own.

The Church of England, if it is to return to reality and survive, must somehow recover the exuberant incoherence of the nineteenth and early twentieth centuries. This wasn't at the time a tranquil condition. Christians were anguished and outraged and even sent each other to jail over questions which have now lost all their force, such as how much an Anglican priest should resemble a Roman Catholic one. Perhaps, in a hundred years' time, today's disagreements over sexuality and feminism will come to seem just as much culture-bound and just as little about the essentials of Christianity. But unless both sides concede – or, better, freely grant – that the other is actually Christian, there will soon be no one but historians to care.

The parties of the Church of England were once mass movements, or mass immobilities, but have now dwindled into clubs for the fanatically like-minded, and for people who enjoy plotting. Yet all the traditional church parties at their best had something which a surviving church will need. The enthusiasm, flexibility and organizational pragmatism of the evangelicals, the love of humanity and the clever interest in the outside world of the liberals, and the slightly unnerving because other-worldly spirituality of the Anglo-Catholics: all these helped the Church engage with the world, and supply things that the world, and not just the most committed churchgoers and clergy, wanted, and recognized that they needed.

The old Church rested on invisible and unpaid women. The new one will have to be sustained by women who are visible, some of whom are paid, and who have other things in their lives as well. The decades of wrangling about whether they are entitled to role and recognition are over, and that's a real victory – perhaps the only one in this story, even though England got there a long time before. Women clergy are by and large wholly uninterested in church parties. This book has been a story of people with no common sense whatsoever. It is possible that women will restore that balance.

The Church is also going to have to reconcile itself with its heritage. It's difficult to overestimate the extent to which the most vigorously intelligent and interesting clergy hate English Heritage Christianity. The vision of a lovely church in a lovely village means to church planners a building that is impossible to heat, endlessly expensive to maintain, and a congregation with varying degrees of commitment which thinks the church belongs to them. All these things are true, but just possibly the congregation has a point.

# NOTES

## Non-acknowledgements

For reasons which the book makes clear, people employed by the Church have to exercise a reasonable caution in speaking out about it. Unless it is essential to the story to give a name to a character who appears in it, we have avoided doing so. We are, nonetheless, extremely grateful to the large number of people who spoke openly to us, and to those who read the manuscript and offered comments.

## Chapter 1

**Page 2**      *Faith in the City* was immediately denounced by one irritated Thatcherite as 'Marxist'. Though this was widely supposed to have been Norman Tebbit, Runcie said years later that he thought it was Peter Lilley, his local MP in St Albans and a keen Christian.

**Page 5**      On **'welfare utopianism'** and the contribution of the Church and church people, see Linda Woodhead, 'Introduction', in Linda Woodhead and Rebecca Catto (eds), *Religion and Change in Modern Britain*, London: Routledge, 2012, pp. 1–33.

**Page 6**      **David Edwards**, *Christian England*, originally published in three volumes (1981–5), and abridged as a single volume, *A Concise History of English Christianity*, London: Fount, 1998.

**Page 10**      By the time of the religious census of 1851, **'dissenters'** accounted for 44 per cent of Sunday church attenders in England. See Robert Currie, Alan Gilbert and Lee Horsley, *Churches and Churchgoers*, Oxford: Clarendon Press, 1977.

**Page 10**      '**... a theological and political middle way**'. In the seventeenth century the Church of England was described as a 'via media' between 'the painted harlot on the hill and the slovenly wench in the valley' (George Herbert), or 'the meretricious gaudiness of the

Church of Rome and the squalid sluttery of fanatic conventicles'
(Bishop Simon Patrick). Cited by Paul Avis, *The Anglican
Understanding of the Church: An Introduction*, 2nd edn, London:
SPCK, 2013, p. 63.

**Page 10** '… **a global model of reasonable and undogmatic Christianity**'.
Anglican confidence had expanded along with the British Empire:
'a divinely ordained British state benefitted internally from the
unifying and civilising power of the state church, while the world-
order gained from the unifying Christian influence of the British
Empire'. John Kent, *William Temple: Church, State and Society in
Britain, 1880–1950*, Cambridge: Cambridge University Press, 1992,
p. 180.

In fact the idea of the Church of England as a moderating and
unifying force conveniently glossed over the suffering caused
by its long struggles to impose unity – burnings in the sixteenth
century, imprisonments in the seventeenth, riots in the eighteenth,
prejudice in the nineteenth. The Church of England 'fought long
and hard to keep its old privileges and, in the process, acted badly
towards all manner of groups within society'. William Whyte,
'What Future for Establishment?', in Mark Chapman, Judith Maltby
and William Whyte (eds), *The Established Church: Past, Present and
Future*, London: T&T Clark, 2011, p. 190.

**Page 11** '**The great social forces**'. 'You cannot fight against the future. Time
is on our side. The great social forces which move onwards in their
might and majesty … are marshalled on our side'. Extract from
William Ewart Gladstone's speech in favour of the Second Reform
Bill of June 1866.

**Page 12** '… **bishops descended through a line of laying on of hands**'.
There were in fact at least two understandings of episcopacy in the
Church of England. According to the first distinctively CofE one, a
bishop is part of the traditional social structure, a state-appointed
'Lord Spiritual' in Parliament. According to the second, more
Catholic, understanding, a bishop is marked out by the charisma of
office transmitted by ritual means in an apostolic succession.

**Page 14** '**Over the next three decades** …' According to the British Social
Attitudes surveys, the number of people identifying as Anglican
fell from almost one in two in 1983 to one in five in 2014 – a
decline, in terms of overall population share, of over half. Within
the same period the number of those saying they have 'no religion'

grew from two in five to one in two. These findings have been confirmed by other surveys, even though they differ from some of the Census findings. For further discussion see Woodhead (2016) 'Why No Religion is the New Religion' http://www.britac.ac.uk/events/2016/Why_no_religion_is_the_new_religion.cfm

**Page 14** '... **bishops and dons**'. Until the 1980s it had been reasonable, as the sociologist David Martin put it, for a member of the Church of England to expect that 'God, the monarchy and Oxford University would act in reasonable conformity' (personal conversation).

# Chapter 2

**Page 16** The First Demographic Transition of c.1870–1945 strengthened marriage and the small family unit; the **Second Demographic Transition**, which began in Britain in the 1960s, weakened them. It involved 'contraceptive revolution, sexual revolution, and gender revolution'. Ron Lesthaeghe, 'The Unfolding Story of the Second Demographic Transition', cited by Callum Brown, *Religion and the Demographic Revolution*, Woodbridge: Boydell Press, 2012, p. 10.

**Page 17** **Cuddesdon College**, later amalgamated with Ripon Hall to become 'Ripon College Cuddesdon', was founded by Bishop Samuel Wilberforce in 1854, the year in which dissenters were admitted to the bachelors' degrees in Oxford. Owen Chadwick, *The Founding of Cuddesdon*, Oxford: Oxford University Press, 1954, p. 1.

**Page 19** '... **most ordinary Anglicans were rather liberal**.'

| Liberal views on abortion, same-sex marriage, euthanasia | Age 18–29 | 30s | 40s | 50s | 60s | 70+ |
|---|---|---|---|---|---|---|
| **Total CofE** | 81% | 71% | 67% | 64% | 57% | 49% |
| **Regular churchgoing CofE** | 62% | 60% | 45% | 42% | 46% | 40% |

Source: Woodhead with YouGov, 2013; http://faithdebates.org.uk/research/

**Page 20** In a narrower sense, '**patronage system**' refers to the historic arrangement whereby parishes are in the gift of formal patrons, of which there are six main types: bishops (the largest group), private patrons (like a landowner), Oxbridge colleges, Crown and Lord Chancellor, Deans and Chapters, Evangelical Patronage Trusts, diocesan boards of patronage. In the broader sense used here, it refers to the whole system of clerical preferment.

**Page 20** 'power ... mostly kept under wraps, but occasionally bursting out in vigorous and unexpected ways'. A paraphrase of Ysenda Maxtone Graham, *The Church Hesitant: A Portrait of the Church of England Today*, London: Hodder & Stoughton, 1993, p. 58.

**Page 23** 'Janie Jones went on the Industrial Relations course'. A. N. Wilson, *Unguarded Hours*, London: Hamlyn, 1983, p. 171.

**Page 24** **Deacon**: probably derived from an obsolete Greek word meaning 'to run on errands'.

**Page 25** The best definitions of the contemporary **tribes** in the Church of England are offered by the spoof 'Archdruid Eileen of the Beaker Folk of Husborne Crawley':

*[Anglo-]Catholic*: Not actually proper Roman Catholic. Cos if we were we wouldn't need to say Catholic. And you wouldn't be looking at our profile, would you, Sandra? If you get the job as our minister we'll call you 'Father' whether you like it or not.

*Evangelical*: We've all sinned. And now we're all much better. But them out there ... oh boy ... God will meet them where they are. And make them like us.

*Liberal*: Tea lights, pebbles, 1970s hymns played on an 1870s organ. We're progressive, we're hip, we're welcoming, we're loose on doctrine and tight on finances. We're the Church of the future. We'll all be dead in 20 years and the building will be a snooker hall.

*Charismatic*: In the 60s we had prophecies, healing and speaking in far-ancient tongues. But we've tidied that down to tweed and Matt Redman.

(http://cyber-coenobites.blogspot.com/2015/02/
church-profiles-some-clues.html)

**Page 26** The '**woman question**': debates about women's status in the Church shifted from being framed, in the eighteenth and nineteenth centuries, in terms of the wider social order, to being framed, in the twentieth and twenty-first centuries, in terms of church order. See Sean Gill,

*Women and the Church of England*, London: SPCK, 1994. The Church was much quicker to abandon its belief in racial difference and complementarity than in gendered difference and complementarity, but as late as 1920 it was still speaking of them in the same breath: 'Race and sex have their respective gifts to be dedicated and used …' *The Ministry of Women: A Report by a Committee Appointed by the Archbishop of Canterbury*, London: SPCK, 1920, p. 9.

**Page 26**     **Dick France** argued that while St Paul might condone women's subordination in the family he didn't want it in church. R. T. France, *Women in the Church's Ministry*, Grand Rapids: Eerdmans, 1995.

**Page 27**     **'women's ordination … would happen soon'.** By the 1970s a majority of Anglicans, including churchgoers, were in favour of women's ordination. For more details see second note for page 78.

**Page 27**     **Mary Daly**, *Beyond God the Father*, Boston: Beacon Press, 1973; Sallie McFague, *Models of God: Theology for an Ecological, Nuclear Age*, Minneapolis: Fortress Press, 1987; **Starhawk**, *The Spiral Dance*, San Francisco: Harper & Row, 1979; **Rosemary Radford Ruether**, *Women-Church: Theology and the Practice of Feminist Liturgical Communities*, San Francisco: Harper and Row, 1985.

**Page 28**     Margaret Webster, one of the founders of **MOW**, tells its story from the inside in *A New Strength, A New Song: The Journey to Women's Priesthood*, London: Mowbray, 1994.

**Page 28**     **'God our mother'.** Janet Morley, 'Collect for Mothering Sunday', from *All Desires Known*, London: SPCK, 1992, p. 11. This first appeared as a pamphlet in 1988.

**Page 32**     **'The academic training was serious'.** Nevertheless, the verdict of Mike Hampson, a contemporary of Linda's in training at Cuddesdon, was that the College's brand of liberalism 'asked all the right questions but offered no answers, which is like knocking everything down then offering no help to build it up again. The tragedy … was that we were never formally taught the positive aspects of a liberal theology … we knew all about what we did not believe.' Ibid., p. 99.

**Page 32**     **'We knew there were problems'.** Mike Hampson, *Last Rites: The End of the Church of England*, London: Granta, 2006, p. 2.

# Chapter 3

Page 40 '… a slim book published pseudonymously in 1970'. Alex Davidson, *The Returns of Love: Letters of a Christian Homosexual*, Downers Grove: Inter-Varsity Press, 1971.

Page 40 'She is a convinced Christian'. Ibid., p. 70.

Page 41 'I suppose one who had the gift'. Ibid., p. 72.

Page 42 'Give me the magnetic needle'. Ibid., p. 18.

Page 43 '… mere hirelings'. Ibid., p. 21.

Page 46 '… he safeguarded the place of conservative evangelicalism'. Despite sharing many important characteristics with American fundamentalists, Stott and most other evangelicals in Britain resisted the label, partly because they had a more positive attitude to the state and the universities. See David Bebbington and David Ceri Jones, *Fundamentalism and Evangelicalism in the UK during the Twentieth Century*, Oxford: Oxford University Press, 2013.

Page 46 'Stott's greatest achievement'. According to McGrath, three main factors led to evangelical renewal in the post-war period – the 'Bash camps' for young men led by E. J. H. Nash, the Inter-Varsity Fellowship Christian Unions, and Stott's ministry. Alister McGrath, *Evangelicalism and the Future of Christianity*, Downers Grove: Inter-Varsity Press, 1995. On Stott's career and influence see Brian Stanley, *The Global Diffusion of Evangelicalism: The Age of Billy Graham and John Stott*, Downers Grove: IVP Academic, 2013.

Page 47 Tony Higton, *That the World May Believe*, London: Marshall Pickering, 1985.

Page 47 'By the end of 1976, 24 people had professed faith in Christ.' Ibid., p. 5.

Page 48 'From a personal point of view I was very sad to see these people leave.' Ibid., p. 15.

Page 51 'Protestantism was no longer a part of English identity as it had been'. On the decline of Protestant influence and identity in England see S. J. D. Green, *The Passing of Protestant England: Secularisation and Social Change c.1920–1960*, Cambridge: Cambridge University Press, 2011.

Page 52    'The fact that the organisation proposed by the Archbishop
           of Canterbury is precisely the same organisation as has been
           adopted by Lenin'. Cited by Kenneth Thompson, *Bureaucracy
           and Church Reform: The Organisational Response of the Church of
           England to Social Change 1800–1965*, Oxford: Oxford University
           Press, 1970, p. 181.

Page 52    'The solution, which appeared in 1919'. Traditionally the Church
           of England had been coextensive with the nation. With the
           Enabling Act of 1919 came the new definition of a member as
           someone baptized into the Church who reports that he or she is a
           member. Contemporaries like Hensley Henson argued that even
           this step reduced the Church to a denomination.

Page 57    Trevor Beeson believes the last straw for **Bennett** was his failure to
           be appointed Dean of Winchester in 1987. Beeson should know,
           since he was appointed instead. *Round the Church in Fifty Years: A
           Personal Journey*, London: SCM, 1997, p. 216.

Page 62    '... evangelicals' hatred of liberals and obsession with moral
           purity'. There are different theories about why the battle against
           homosexuality became such a central and defining one for
           evangelicalism from the 1980s. Stephen Bates argues that, having
           failed to win the battle against women's ordination, evangelicals were
           looking for another cause to rally around; Kristin Aune believes the
           struggle is really about the defence of a certain kind of 'hegemonic
           masculinity' (which also helps explain why evangelicals don't bother
           much about lesbianism); others think it is the final frontier in the
           battle to defend biblical inerrancy. All these theories are probably
           true. Stephen Bates, *A Church at War: Anglicans and Homosexuality*,
           London: Hodder & Stoughton, 2005; Kristin Aune, 'Between
           Subordination and Sympathy: Evangelical Christians, Masculinity,
           and Gay Sexuality', in Stephen Hunt (ed.), *Contemporary Christianity
           and LGBT Sexualities*, Aldershot: Ashgate, 2009, pp. 39–49.

# Chapter 4

Page 64    '... 90 per cent of the British population subscribed to a liberal set
           of values'. This figure comes from population surveys carried out by
           Woodhead with YouGov (2013) and available at http://faithdebates.

org.uk/research/. On the methodology and analysis (with Bernard Silverman) see Linda Woodhead (ed.), *What British People Really Believe*, Special issue of *Modern Believing*, Vol. 55, No. 1, 2014.

**Page 65** 'Bishops are a part of English culture'. T. S. Eliot, *Notes Towards the Definition of Culture*, New York: Harcourt Brace, 1949, p. 31.

**Page 66** The distinction between **church and sect** comes from the great sociologist of religion, Ernst Troeltsch. The 'church type' holds a sacred canopy over the whole life of a society, and resists systematic rationalization in theology and organization. The 'sect type' aspires after purity, personal perfection and close fellowship between members of tight-knit groups, sharply distinguishing itself from 'the world'. Later sociologists added the category of 'denomination' to refer to a church which accepts the legitimacy of other churches in the same society. Kenneth Thompson, *Bureaucracy and Church Reform*, proposes the category of 'Ecclesia' to describe the Church of England, which falls between a world church (e.g. Roman Catholic) and a denomination (e.g. the Episcopal Church of the USA). Ernst Troeltsch, *The Social Teaching of the Christian Churches*, 2 vols, London: George Allen & Unwin; New York: Macmillan, 1931 (originally 1911). For an account of how these different 'types' have played out in Christian history see Linda Woodhead, *A Very Short Introduction to Christianity*, 2nd edn, rev., Oxford: Oxford University Press, 2014.

**Page 66** Anna Strhan, *Aliens and Strangers? The Struggle for Coherence in the Everyday Lives of Evangelicals*, Oxford: Oxford University Press, 2015.

**Page 67** Pierre Bourdieu, *Pascalian Meditations*, Cambridge: Polity Press, 2000.

# Chapter 5

**Page 74** Women's 'works of benevolence'. On laywomen's work in the Church prior to the Second World War see, for example, Sean Gill, *Women and the Church of England*, op. cit.; Henrietta Blackmore (ed.), *The Beginning of Women's Ministry: The Revival of the Deaconess in the Nineteenth-Century Church of England*, London: Boydell Press, 2007; Frank Prochaska, *Christianity and Social Service in Modern Britain*, Oxford: Oxford University Press, 2006.

**Page 75**  '… **the nourishing soup**'. Barbara Pym, *A Glass of Blessings* [1958], London: Virago (2009), p. 19.

**Page 76**  On the **matrifocal family** as the basic unit of religion and local society in England see Tim Jenkins, *Religion in English Everyday Life: An Ethnographic Approach*, New York: Berghahn, 1999.

**Page 76**  'I **mean, me divorce**'. Ellen Clark-King, *Theology by Heart: Women, the Church and God*, Peterborough: Epworth Press, 2004, p. 76.

**Page 76**  'In **the old days**'. Ibid., p. 146.

**Page 78**  '**A lot of people seem to think**'. Ibid., p. 10.

**Page 78**  '**Over 80 per cent of Anglicans**'. The 1979 *Now!* Religion Survey found that 85 per cent of self-identified Anglicans thought that 'women should be able to become members of the clergy'. Ben Clements, 'Changing Attitudes towards Gender Equality and the Ordination of Women', in Linda Woodhead (ed.), *What British People Really Believe*, Special issue of *Modern Believing*, Vol. 55, No.1, 2014, pp. 16–21.

**Page 79**  '**How long can you cripple the church …?**' Jonathan Petre, *By Sex Divided: The Church of England and Women Priests*, London: Fount/HarperCollins, 1994, p. 58.

**Page 80**  On **Ronald Hall**, see David M. Paton, *R.O.: The Life and Times of Bishop Ronald Hall of Hong Kong*, Diocese of Hong Kong and Macao, 1985.

**Page 81**  '… **unable to express any opinion**'. http://www.womenpriests.org/related/rose_08.asp.

**Page 84**  'It **was like a submarine**'. Petre, *By Sex Divided*, p. 160.

**Page 87**  '… **a generous financial package**'. Priests who left between 1994 and 2004 were provided with compensation amounting to a full stipend in year one, three-quarters in year two, and two-thirds in year three; http://www.hmrc.gov.uk/manuals/nimmanual/nim02630.htm.

**Page 87**  **Ordinariate**: in *total*, the number of Church of England clergy who 'crossed over to Rome' between 1994 and 2014 is calculated by Woodhead as just under 400, of which about 100 joined the Ordinariate. There was also traffic in the other direction, but the number is not available. *The Tablet*, News, 1 August 2014; http://www.thetablet.co.uk/news/1028/0/new-figures-show-almost-400-catholic-priests-were-anglicans.

**Page 89** '… **clergymen … seemed to hate them so much**'. Refusing communion from women, spitting on them, asking whether they were menstruating – these were some of the practices reported to us, and real misogyny of this kind was also experienced first-hand by Linda in the early 1990s. It is unflinchingly described by Maggi Dawn in *Like the Wideness of the Sea: Women Bishops and the Church of England*, London: Darton, Longman and Todd, 2013.

**Page 89** '**In Britain the children of Anglicans…**' The 2013 British Social Attitudes Survey shows that there is a 40 per cent chance that those raised Christian will lose that affiliation. By contrast 90 per cent of those raised with no religion remain that way.

**Page 89** '**But the biggest casualty of the battle over women was the continuing support of ordinary English women.**' On the significance of women's defection for church decline see Callum Brown, *The Death of Christian Britain: Understanding Secularisation, 1800–2000*, London: Routledge, and Linda Woodhead: 'Gendering Secularisation Theory', *Social Compass* 55 (2), June 2008, pp. 189–95. For a period, the ordination of women nevertheless saved the Church of England from a crisis of falling clergy numbers: by 2012 one in five stipendiary clergy were women, and over half of all non-stipendiary/self-supporting clergy. The typical woman clergyperson is unpaid and middle-aged, but this pattern is unlikely to be sustained. And younger women are not being attracted into ministry: in 2012, 71 per cent of the candidates aged under 40 recommended for training were male. Linda Woodhead, 'Not Enough Boots on the Ground', in Malcolm Doney (ed.), *How Healthy is the C of E?* London: Canterbury Press, 2014, pp. 50–4.

# Chapter 6

**Page 91** Inexplicably, Carey opens a chapter of his autobiography with the **Dickinson** poem. *Know the Truth: A Memoir*, London: Harper Perennial, 2005.

**Page 92** Mrs Thatcher '**was later said to be disappointed in how [Carey] turned out**'. Reported by Eliza Filby, *God and Mrs Thatcher*, London: Biteback, 2015.

**Page 92-3** On the full process of Carey's **selection** see Simon Lee and Peter Stanford, *Believing Bishops*, London: Faber & Faber, 1990.

**Page 93**    **John Bickersteth.** A delightful series of photographs of five
generations of the hereditary priestly clan of Bickersteths (four
bishops and one canon) is reproduced in the centrefold of Douglas
Davies and Mathew Guest's *Bishops, Wives and Children: Spiritual
Capital Across Generations*, Aldershot: Ashgate, 2007.

**Page 94**    'The Church's decline'. There are numerous collections of statistics
on the decline of the Church of England in the UK in many easily
available sources. The most comprehensive for 1700–1970 is Robert
Currie, Alan Gilbert and Lee Horsley, *Churches and Churchgoers*,
Oxford: Clarendon Press, 1977. Peter Brierley's regular English
Church Censuses then take up the story. The most up-to-date
source is the website 'British Religion in Numbers' (www.brin.
ac.uk), maintained by the indefatigable Dr Clive Field. These and
other sources show that there was nothing new about the Church's
decline, which had been ongoing for over a century before Carey
called for a Decade of Evangelism. There had been a slow and gradual
decline since the 1870s, followed by a rapid one since the 1970s.
Between 1970 and 1989 the Church of England as a going concern
was effectively reduced to not much more than half its previous size.
The rate of decline has not reduced since then.By 1997 usual Sunday
church attendance had fallen below the symbolically significant level
of one million.

**Page 96**    'Hardly anyone in the Church understands the whole of it'.
Concerning the structure of the Church, Kenneth Thompson's
*Bureaucracy and Church Reform: The Organisational Response of
the Church of England to Social Change 1800–1965*, Oxford: Oxford
University Press, 1970 provides essential background, offering
a brilliant analysis of the formative stages of the 'organisational
revolution' which changed the Church of England, like many
other institutions, from a traditional structure to that of a modern
bureaucracy over the course of the nineteenth and twentieth centuries.

**Page 96**    **Dioceses**: the power of dioceses, which had historically been
small, was swollen by the state's general post-Second World War
policy of decentralization, including of finance. Ibid., pp. 227–8.

**Page 98**    **Parliament**: on Parliament's growing indifference to the Church of
England see R. M. Morris, *Church and State in 21st Century Britain:
The Future of Church Establishment*, Basingstoke: Palgrave, 2009.

**Page 99**    The authoritative study of the **Church Commissioners**, and the
crisis in 1992, is Andrew Chandler's *The Church of England in the*

*Twentieth Century: The Church Commissioners and the Politics of Reform, 1948–1998*, Woodbridge: The Boydell Press, 2006.

**Page 99** The '**Bounty**' was established in 1704 when Queen Anne set up a corporation to receive her revenues from first fruits and tithes and apply them to the augmentation of the incomes of impoverished clergy. On this and the merging with the Ecclesiastical Commission see Thompson, *Bureaucracy and Church Reform*, pp. 56–90 and Chandler, *The Church of England*, pp. 7–32.

**Page 103** The clergy's financial deal '**kept getting better**'. In the decade after 1970 the stipends of diocesan bishops increased by 79 per cent. In the 1980s clergy stipends increased by 74 per cent above inflation, and pensions had been raised by 120 per cent above inflation on the back of clergy stipends and national insurance increases. Chandler, Ibid., pp. 261, 389.

**Page 104** '**... people sighed and dug deeper**'. Parish giving rose steadily each year from about £50m in 1993 to £952m in 2013; https://www.churchofengland.org/media/2265027/2013financestatistics.pdf.

**Page 106** The **Turnbull Commission** consisted of sixteen men and but one woman. It was accompanied by another commission (the Bridge Commission) which reviewed synodical government. Both reports were critical of Synod and of the Committees in Church House. A thorough spring-clean was being prepared. *Working as One Body: The Report of the Archbishops' Commission on the Organisation of the Church of England*, London, 1995.

**Page 108** 'It could fairly be said to represent nothing except itself'. Chandler, *The Church of England*, p. 478.

**Page 109** '**Reaction was generally positive**'. Carey, *Know the Truth*, p. 174.

**Page 109** "**I've just seen the Archbishop of Canterbury's diary for 1993**". Maxtone Graham, *The Church Hesitant*, p. 234.

**Page 109** *Issues in Human Sexuality* was produced by a small group chaired by John Austin Baker, Bishop of Salisbury. The other members were Richard Harries, Bishop of Oxford, John Lucas the conservative Oxford philosopher, and William Persson the evangelical Bishop of Doncaster. When the document was nearly finalised, John Austin Baker said he could not go along with it, as he now believed the Church should affirm gay relationships. He would therefore drop out or sign a dissenting note. In the end, the rest of the group persuaded him to sign. Before long, *Issues* *in Human Sexuality* was being used by some bishops to screen out gay candidates. Mike Hampson recalls a bishop calling him in to ask if he was having sexual relations with his male partner, and declining to appoint him when he would make no comment. Hampson comments, 'The price of tolerance for gay clergy rose that day from "don't tell" to "pledge celibacy", or possibly tell a barefaced lie.' Hampson, *Last Rites*, p. 162.

**Page 109** 'This kind of self-deception'. It was also around this time that Church of England communications started to get into the business of 'spinning' news about the Church. The distinguished religious correspondent for the *Daily Telegraph*, Clifford Longley, was appalled: 'The primary responsibility of an honest press officer is to openness and to the truth, good, bad or indifferent, not the suppression of facts or the "talking up" of a particular trend.' Clifford Longley, *Church Times*, 30 January 1999.

**Page 111** '... Carey took refuge in a managerial voodoo'. 'Looking back on the ferment of the 1990s and all the changes which were introduced, I have no regrets about any decisions I made ... I can take some satisfaction in the creation of the Archbishops' Council ... The essential shape of what was achieved will continue to serve the Church well for decades to come.' Carey, *Know the Truth*, p. 175.

**Page 111** Scepticism about the '**Decade of Evangelism**'. David Edwards commented acerbically that a 'Decade of Thinking' about the Church, its problems, and its relation to society would be a better idea (Letter to the *Church Times*, 25 June 1999). He might have recalled Hensley Henson, who said in 1926: 'When I was a parish clergyman, it was generally said, and I think, with substantial truth, that missions were "superfluous in a well-worked parish, and mischievous in an ill-worked one".' *Letters*, London: SPCK, 1951, p. 47.

# Chapter 7

**Page 113** '**The most astonishing development in twentieth-century Christianity came like a thief in the night**'. 'Let's have a feeling of wrappedaroundness,' said Gavin Reid, introducing a musical event for youth fellowships in 1976. Pete Ward, *Growing up Evangelical*,

London: SPCK, 1996, p. 80. On the global charismatic movement see Allan Anderson, *To the Ends of the Earth: Pentecostalism and the Transformation of World Christianity*, New York: Oxford University Press, 2013.

**Page 115** '... [gives] the lie to the suspicion'. Sarah Coakley, *God, Sexuality and the Self*, Cambridge: Cambridge University Press, 2013, p. 174.

**Page 116** **John Wimber**, a former rock musician and Quaker, exercised leadership within the Vineyard group of churches, of which the Toronto Airport Church, which 'invented' the eponymous blessing, was one. Stanley, *The Global Diffusion of Evangelicalism*, pp. 205–9.

**Page 117** On **Billy Graham** and his impact in Britain see Callum Brown, *Religion and Society in Twentieth-Century Britain*, London: Longman, 2006, and Stanley, *The Global Diffusion of Evangelicalism*.

**Page 124** On the **Toronto Blessing** see David Hilborn (ed.), *'Toronto' in Perspective: Papers on the New Charismatic Wave of the Mid-1990s*, Carlisle: Paternoster Press; Jürgen Römer, *The Toronto Blessing*, Abo: Abo Akademi University Press, 2002; Martyn Percy, *Words, Wonders and Powers: Understanding Contemporary Christian Fundamentalism and Revivalism*, London: SPCK, 1996.

**Page 125** '... the "charismatic evangelicals", as they had now become'. Mike Hampson argues on the basis of his own experience that the merger of evangelicalism and the charismatic movement since the early 1980s degraded the charismatic movement. He reflects wistfully on: 'the silence, wonder, reverence and awe at the mystery of God ... when the charismatic phenomena were spontaneous and shared, not delivered on cue at specified events like the Alpha Course's Holy Spirit Day ... Humility and a sense of community saved the movement from folly and excess.' Hampson, *Last Rites*, pp. 92–3.

**Page 126** '... in the wider evangelical movement ... a clear division'. By the new millennium there were three broad categories of evangelical in Britain: 'Reformed' evangelicals of a Calvinistic temper (represented by the Church Society [1835] and after 1993 by Reform), 'Charismatic' evangelicals, and 'Open' evangelicals (represented, after 2003, by Fulcrum). From the 1970s Charismatic evangelicalism had been further embedded by way of the Christian festivals, including Greenbelt, Spring Harvest and New Wine.

'Post-evangelicalism' emerged in the 1990s, given its manifesto by Dave Tomlinson's *The Post-Evangelical*, London: SPCK, 1995. See Rob Warner, *Reinventing English Evangelicalism, 1966–2001*, Milton Keynes: Paternoster Press, 2007.

Page 126   '... charismatic evangelical Anglicanism had two real and lasting successes'. By 2014 a third of Church of England clergy identified as evangelicals. In Synod the proportion of evangelicals was probably higher. Among churchgoers it may be around a quarter, and among Anglicans as a whole around 10 per cent. Greg Smith, *21st Century Evangelicals*, Watford: Instant Apostle, 2015; Linda Woodhead, survey of Anglican clergy, results available at http://faithdebates.org.uk/wp-content/uploads/2014/10/Clergy-survey-Press-Release.pdf.

Page 127   '... circles of affluent "home counties" English middle classes'. By the twenty-first century white British evangelicals were pretty uniformly middle class and affluent: 71 per cent were professionals, and nearly all were wealthy. Smith, *21st Century Evangelicals*, p. 21.

Page 127   'Coakley recorded such tensions in two churches'. Coakley, *God, Sexuality, and the Self*, pp. 164–84.

Page 128   **David Pytches**, *Does God Speak Today?* London: Hodder & Stoughton, 1989.

Page 132   'Sociologists ... a kind of public utility'. Grace Davie, *Religion in Britain since 1945: Believing without Belonging*, Oxford: Blackwell, 1994; Grace Davie, *Religion in Britain: A Persistent Paradox*, Oxford: Wiley-Blackwell, 2015.

# Chapter 8

Page 135   '... the Lambeth Conference of 1998, a three-week gathering of all the Anglican bishops in the world'. The conference was attended by nearly 750 bishops, including 224 from Africa, 177 from the US and Canada, 139 from the UK and Europe, 95 from Asia, 56 from Australia, 41 from Central and South America, and 4 from the Middle East. Miranda K. Hassett, *The Anglican Communion in Crisis: How Episcopal Dissidents and their African Allies are Reshaping Anglicanism*, Princeton: Princeton University

Press, 2007, p. 71. On the history of the Anglican Communion
see Kevin Ward, *A History of Global Anglicanism*, Cambridge:
Cambridge University Press, 2006.

**Page 135**  **Carey's cheerful recollection of Lambeth 1998:** 'The day was bright
with a gentle breeze as purple-cassocked bishops, including eleven
women, and other delegates processed into the mother church of the
Anglican Communion. Hundreds of children waved blue and gold
banners, while the cathedral's fourteen bells rang out their welcome.
His Royal Highness the Prince of Wales, our principal guest, was
slightly delayed because of animal-rights demonstrators as well as a
noisy group of homosexual activists.' *Know the Truth*, p. 319.

**Page 144**  **'The American conservatives ... reappeared in 1998 with
massive reinforcements'.** The conservative preparations for
Lambeth 1998 are documented by Stephen Bates, *A Church at
War: Anglicans and Homosexuality*, London: I.B.Tauris, 2004.

**Page 146**  **'... wealthy Americans and Australians'.** The important role
of the ultra-conservative Sydney diocese is documented by
Hassett, *Anglican Communion in Crisis* and Muriel Porter, *Sydney
Anglicans and the Threat to World Anglicanism*, Aldershot:
Ashgate, 2011.

**Page 146**  **'... their detestation of homosexuality'.** Wider popular attitudes
to homosexuality in Africa seem in fact to be rather mixed.
Although there is no reliable statistical evidence, qualitative
studies find variety both within African countries and between
them. See Kevin Ward, 'The Role of the Anglican and Catholic
Churches in Uganda in Public Discourse on Homosexuality
and Ethics', in *Journal of Eastern African Studies*, January 2015,
9 (1), pp. 127–44, and Hassett, *Anglican Communion in Crisis*.
Hassett mounts a convincing case against the idea, much fortified
by Philip Jenkins' *The Next Christendom* (2011), that there is
such a thing as 'southern' Christianity, and that it is any more
homogeneously conservative than 'northern' is liberal. What
she demonstrates is that in an age of globalization conservative
evangelicals across the world were able to enter into partnership
and make common cause.

**Page 149**  **'Carey's instinct was to deny that there was any problem with
homosexuality among the clergy'.** In his autobiography he quotes
Wolfhart Pannenberg's assertion that a church which did not
treat homosexual activity as a departure from the biblical norm

'would cease to be the one, holy Catholic and apostolic Church', and comments approvingly: 'I was convinced he was right, and I was determined to resist any move that might make our great Communion take a step in that direction.' *Know the Truth*, p. 313.

Page 150    **'Those who are supporting [homosexuality]'.** Hassett, *Anglican Communion in Crisis*, p. 79.

Page 150    **A 'test case for Anglican unity'.** Carey, *Know the Truth*, p. 333.

Page 150    **'We are now in a genuinely evil situation'.** Jeffrey John, quoted in Bates, *A Church at War*, p. 164.

Page 156    **'"yet to face the intellectual revolution of Copernicus and Einstein"'** Jack Spong, quoted by Hassett in *Anglican Communion in Crisis*, p. 72.

# Chapter 9

Page 157    **'Understanded of the common people'.** Tyndale and the other early translators of the Bible into English sought to produce versions which were 'understanded of the common people'.

Page 158    **'... a congregation without a church'.** Cole Moreton attributes the quote to Andrew Marr, who said that the space in front of Kensington Palace had become 'an outdoor cathedral, its congregation led by no one but themselves'. Cole Moreton, *Is God Still an Englishman? How Britain Lost Its Faith (But Found New Soul)*, London: Abacus, 2010, p. 126.

Page 160    **'... tightly written, pen driving into the cheap paper'.** Rowan Williams, *Open to Judgement: Sermons and Addresses*, new edition, London: Darton, Longman and Todd, p. 112.

Page 162    **'... even his most admiring biographer'.** Rupert Shortt, *Rowan's Rule*, new edition, London: Hodder & Stoughton, 2014.

Page 164    **'... Rowan's supporters did their best to blame Richard Harries.'** See John Peart-Binns, *A Heart in my Head: A Biography of Richard Harries*, London: Continuum, 2007. The fullest account of the Jeffrey John affair is found in Stephen Bates, *A Church at* War, ch. 10.

Page 168    **'the reasons for which he eventually said "no"'.** After the Jeffrey John decision, Rowan told the House of Bishops that 'the reasons for which he eventually came to say "No" were the same reasons for which he'd originally said "Yes" and these were about the wellbeing of the church'. Andrew Goddard, *Rowan Williams: His Legacy*, Oxford: Lion Books, 2nd edn, 2013, p. 104.

Page 169   **'Nor were his enemies satisfied with their victory.'** It was as a direct result of the Jeffrey John affair that three campaigning movements concerned with homosexuality came into being: Inclusive Church, Anglican Mainstream, and Fulcrum. They set the poles of debate and division thereafter, being respectively pro-gay, fiercely anti-gay, and politely anti-gay.

Page 175   Goddard calculates that Rowan's talk on **Sharia** has 6,000 words but only 132 sentences, an average of 47 words per sentence. Goddard, *Rowan Williams*, p. 234.

Page 177   **'The Sharia debacle ...'** Rowan never felt the need to apologize for his remarks on Sharia. In a speech to Synod a few days later he said he must 'take responsibility for any unclarity', but concluded: 'if we can attempt to speak for the liberties and consciences of others in this country as well as our own, we shall I believe be doing something we as a Church are called to do in Christ's name, witnessing to his Lordship and not compromising it'. Later he said, 'I didn't feel any lasting damage was done.' In trying to exonerate Rowan from blame for the Sharia debacle, his biographer only makes things worse: 'Although causing incomprehension and outrage within wider society, the lecture is perfectly consonant with the whole direction of his teaching as archbishop.' Goddard, *Rowan Williams*, pp. 233, 239.

# Chapter 10

Page 179   **'I think Rowan basically made decisions alone'.** Peter Selby, cited by Goddard, *Rowan Williams*, p. 294.

Page 181   **'The Church Commissioners didn't help.'** 'To put it bluntly [the Church of England] has subsidised [its] own long-term decline.' Robin Gill, *Vision of Growth*, London: SCM, 1994, p. 85.

Page 182   **'*The Spiritual Revolution*'.** Paul Heelas and Linda Woodhead, *The Spiritual Revolution*, Oxford: Blackwell, 2005.

**Page 187** '... bishops of the "safe rather than sorry" variety'. Trevor
Beeson, who offers portraits of forty-eight bishops from 1832–
2000, concludes that 'virtually all of today's bishops fall into the
category of pastoral-manager, with the strongest emphasis on
manager', and that 'the Church of England entered the twenty-first
century with an alarming lack of bishops of widely acknowledged
ability'. *The Bishops*, London: SCM, 2002, pp. 1, 6.

**Page 190** For a profile of the growing proportion of British people reporting
'**no religion**', see Woodhead, '"No Religion" is the New Religion',
http://faithdebates.org.uk/wp-content/uploads/2014/01/WFD-
No-Religion.pdf.

**Page 192** '**... the historic state churches of Denmark, Norway and Sweden,
retained much higher levels ...**'.

*Statistical Comparison of the Church of England and the Church of Denmark*:

|                                      | CofE (2013)                               | CofD (2014)             | *Note*            |
| ------------------------------------ | ----------------------------------------- | ----------------------- | ----------------- |
| Baptism                              | 12%                                       | 64%                     | % live births     |
| Weddings                             | 20%                                       | 34%                     | % all weddings    |
| Funerals                             | 33%                                       | 83%                     | % all funerals    |
| Sunday attendance                    | 1.5%                                      | 2%                      | % of population   |
| Self-identification/ affiliation     | c.30%                                     | 77% (pay church tax)    | % of population   |
| Christmas                            | 4.5% (Christmas Eve & Christmas Day)      | 20% (evening only)      | % of population   |

Sources for Denmark: http://www.km.dk/folkekirken/
kirkestatistik/; for church attendance, see Marie Vejrup Nielsen
and Hans Raun Iversen (eds), *Tal om kirken: Undersøgelser af
Folkekirkens aktivitets-og deltagerstatistik*, Publikationer fra Det
Teologiske Fakultet 57, 2014.

Source for UK: Church of England, *Statistics for Mission
2013*, London: Archbishops' Council, 2014. https://www.
churchofengland.org/media/2112070/2013statisticsformission.pdf.

**Page 194** 'And finally, Lord, regarding the General Election …' Maxtone
Graham, *Church Hesitant*, p. 206.

**Page 194** '… it just added more words'. One lay person told Maxtone
Graham that the only time in a whole year of churchgoing he had
managed to pray properly was during the two minutes' silence on
Remembrance Day (Ibid. p. 209). The public is thought to require
a constant stream of words. Anglo-Catholicism knew more about
how to pray well, but has failed to spread its influence through
the Church. Giuseppe Giordan and Linda Woodhead (eds), *A
Sociology of Prayer*, Aldershot: Ashgate, 2015.

**Page 194** '… good sermon … few and far between'. In the 1980s Ysenda
Maxtone Graham listened to the most famous preachers in the Church,
from John Stott to Nicky Gumbel, Graham Cray to John MacQuarrie.
She was not impressed: 'It is astonishing how many sermons are less
good than you hoped … Our expectations of sermons are now so
low that we applaud silently to one another if a sermon manages to be
concise and honest'. Maxtone Graham, *The Church Hesitant*, pp. 75–92.

**Page 195** '… urban churches overall were faring even more disastrously
than rural ones'. In 2015 a Church of England report on the
rural church found that two-thirds of parishes and churches were
rural, and just under half the clergy. They account for 40 per cent
of Church of England attendance. More urban churches were
declining than rural ones, and the same number are growing. See
https://www.churchofengland.org/media/2148423/gspercent
20miscpercent201092percent20-percent20ruralpercent20multiper
cent20parishpercent20benefices.pdf.

**Page 195** 'The Church would look a lot more attractive'. Monica Furlong,
*The C of E: The State It's In*, London: SPCK, 2000, p. 382.

**Page 196** '… a majority of Anglicans still voted Conservative'. In the 2015
election 46 per cent of Anglican respondents voted Conservative,
30 per cent Labour, 13 per cent UKIP, 8 per cent Liberal
Democrat, 3 per cent other party. *British Election Study*, 2015
Panel Study, wave 6, available at http://www.britishelectionstudy.
com/data-objects/panel-study-data/

**Page 200** The 'Anglican Covenant'. Philip Giddings, long-serving member
of the Archbishops' Council and a chair of the General Synod's
House of Laity, pointed out that 'When you are having your first
big row is not the time to make the rules you don't have but now
need'. Cited by Goddard, *Rowan Williams*, p. 167. See also Mark

Chapman (ed.), *The Anglican Covenant: Unity and Diversity in the Anglican Communion*, London and New York: Mowbray, 2008.

**Page 200** '… **Rowan would not make any serious attempt to expel**'. The Windsor Report of 2004, by a Lambeth commission set up by the Archbishop, called for a threefold moratorium: on gay bishops, the blessing of same-sex unions, and cross-border incursions. It was defied on every point, as recorded in the headline by Stephen Bates: 'Bishops to Primate: Drop Dead'.

**Page 202** '… **beginning to model something for the Church Catholic**'. Goddard, *Rowan Williams*, p. 121.

# Chapter 11

**Page 206** '**Big buildings and big institutions** …' Address to Bishops' Council, 20-21 March 2012, cited in Andrew Atherstone, 'Archbishop Justin Welby'.

**Page 212** '… **what was now left of the institution they had marched through?**' As well as precipitous decline, a statistical profile of the Church of England in 2015 reported that: If congregations in England consisted of a hundred people: fifty-nine would be female, eleven would be children aged eleven or younger, nineteen would be aged seventy-six or older, seven would be minority ethnic Anglican. There are six adults in church to every one child or young person; https://www.churchofengland.org/media/2261061/everyonecounts_keyfindings.pdf.

**Page 212** '**Things could not go on … How could they be changed?**' Between the 1970s and 2000 the Church of England commissioned several very good reports (including the Morley, Tiller, and Osborne Reports) which did not shy away from the challenges, and proposed sensible and serious reforms. They were not acted upon.

**Page 213** '… **compared with its closest historical cousins, the churches of Denmark, Norway and Sweden, the Church of England did worse**'. See note for Page 192.

**Page 218** '… **over half of the clergy feel that their talents are not recognized or supported**'. A finding from a random-sample survey of 1,509 Anglican clergy listed in *Crockford's* carried out by Woodhead/YouGov in 2014. Data tables and analysis available at http://faithdebates.org.uk/research/

# Some last words:

'Many great British institutions have faced crisis, but only the Church of England has created a situation where virtually all its energy is invested in self-defeating pursuits at every level of the organisation.' Hampson, *Last Rites*, p. 1.

'Christian hatred is powerful because it arises out of deep convictions which really matter to the haters.' Maxtone Graham, *The Church Hesitant*, p. 115.

'Fanatical clergy exist at extreme ends of the spectrum, but in the middle, calm and diligent people are trying to get on with their jobs. Bad-tempered laypeople exist, disrupting the PCC and thriving on church politics, but the average churchgoer is a good sort, trying hard to become a better sort.' Maxtone Graham, *The Church Hesitant*, p. 241.

'The great irony of the present situation is that this need for a highly active, aware and responsive laity comes at a time when the central structures of the church are moving in the opposite direction, towards a controlling clerical oligarchy ... The world picks up the condescension built into the old system (and rediscovered in the new) and will have none of it.' Furlong, *The C of E*, p. 374.

'There is little which is specifically Protestant in the surviving folk religion of England: personal reading of the Bible in the home, anti-popery, familiarity with *Pilgrim's Progress*, these things have simply faded away. There is, on the other hand, much that is decidedly Catholic, both of a traditional and a contemporary kind. It is the medieval, rather than the post-Reformation, religious heritage which remains just alive today.' Adrian Hastings, *A History of English Christianity 1920–1990*, 3rd edn, London: SCM, 1991, p. 666.

'The English God appeared to be dead, but it wasn't true. He was just regenerating. The obstinate way in which people refuse to stop believing has given Him new energy, but He has also changed so much ... the new English God wants us to work with nature ... believes in fair play and good versus evil, but also in free choice, mutual respect, equality ... I'm not advocating this picture of God, only describing the deity that seems to inhabit the minds and imaginations of the English now and informs our cultures, whether we're conscious of Him or not, and whatever we call Him. Or Her. Or Them.' Moreton, *Is God Still an Englishman?*, p. 345.

# INDEX